# ADAM'S RIB
*Essays on Biblical Medicine*

# ADAM'S RIB
## Essays on Biblical Medicine

### Simon S. Levin

M.B., M.R.C.P., D.C.H.
*Johannesburg*

*Geron-X, Inc., Los Altos, California*

220.861
L578

ISBN 0–87672–006–8
Library of Congress Catalog Card No. 78–111609

Printed in the United States of America by
The Colonial Press Inc., Clinton, Mass.

*In memory of my mother
who has been gathered unto her people,
and for my father
who ordered a callow matriculant
Be a doctor!*

## PREFACE

In the United States and Britain there are professional organizations exploring the connections between medicine and religion. These bodies run no study courses and offer no diplomas. Accordingly other diplomas will have to serve as qualifications and credentials in this field. It happens that the medical letters I use behind my name serve equally well in another capacity: Does M.B. mean Bachelor of Medicine? Why not also credits in Biblical Medicine? M.R.C.P. may indicate Membership of the Royal College of Physicians but could be twisted to read Member of the Religious College of Physicians. A Diploma in Child Health could be utilized to mean Diploma in Clinical Hermeneutics, i.e. Biblical exegesis.

These are high and unique qualifications, and armed with such versatile diplomas I feel entitled to contribute some essays on Biblical medicine.

Some of the material in this book has already appeared in various medical journals. The editors of the following journals have kindly given permission for reproduction: *The South African Medical Journal, Medical Proceedings, Central African Journal of Medicine, Journal of Obstetrics and Gynaecology of the British Empire, The Practitioner.*

# CONTENTS

# THE ANATOMY OF GENESIS

"In the beginning God created the heaven and the earth."
It would be difficult to construct a more exalted pronouncement on the universe than is expressed by these mighty
words.

The beginning of the heavens is the uttermost mystery,
but the birth of the earth is thought by many scientists to
have been about 5,000 million years ago. Life itself appeared
some 3,000 million years later, while primitive man left the
trees for a terrestrial future close to 2 million years ago.

It would be fair to say that the enlightened clergy of
the world now accept such time epochs. But earlier divines
had thought otherwise. Archbishop Ussher of Ireland, together with Cambridge Hebraist Dr. John Lightfoot, won
eternal fame about 1650 by calculating that the earth was
created on Sunday morning 23rd October 4,004 B.C.E. Their
date went unchallenged for 100 years.

But then came Darwin, and the geologists, and the
astrophysicists, and much clerical effort was directed towards
harmonizing Genesis with Science. The good bishop had
evidently erred in regarding the days as days instead of
epochs, and why, if one looked carefully (but not too carefully!), one could even detect biological evolution in the
stories of Genesis.

*1*

But it would be wrong to project our modern conceptions on the archaic Hebrew story tellers. As far as possible we should attempt to view their universe through their eyes.

The early Hebrews probably visualized a God hovering over a massive, dark, desolate earthy platform entirely surrounded by water. By a simple fiat of God's will a layer of platform was peeled off to form a firmament above the new surface of the earthy disc, thus dividing the waters above the earth from those below. Both earth and firmament were then fixed by mountainous pillars on the horizon, these plunging down to form as well the foundations of the earth (1 Sam. 2:8, 2 Sam. 22:16, Job 9:6, 26:11, 38:4–6, Ps. 75:3).

The waters above the earth are called in all languages "the sky" or "the heavens," but Hebrew has retained the term *shamayim,* literally, "up there is water."

The firmament was a distant solid layer keeping out the upper waters, which could, however, seep in through the windows (Gen. 7:11) or doors (Ps. 78:23) of heaven to produce snow, hail, cloud, rain or dew. In Hebrew, Greek and Latin, the term "firmament" is derived from roots meaning "firm" or "solid."

Just within the firmament there circulated as well the sun, moon, planets (2 Kings 23:5) and stars, while the highest heavens lay above the starry firmament (Isa. 14:13). Notwithstanding Gen. 1:17, the heavenly bodies were not visualized as causal agents of day or night, but as objects to inspire, mystify and delight the people of the earth. When need be, the sun might even stand still, as it did for Joshua over Gibeon, while the moon tarried over the valley of Ajalon (Josh. 10:12,13). "The stars in their courses fought against Sisera" (Judg. 5:20). A sundial turned back ten degrees for the sake of Hezekiah (2 Kings 20:11).

Though the sun ruled the day, and the moon the night, light was independent of the sun, having been present as a

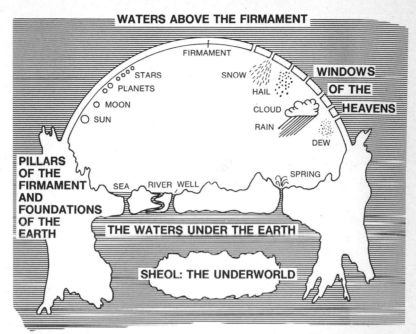

## HEBREW CONCEPTION OF THE WORLD

consequence of divine fiat before the sun was created (Gen. 1:3–5,16). "The day is thine, the night also is thine: thou hast prepared the light and the sun" (Ps. 74:16).

The earth was visualized as a solid, firm disc (Ps. 93:1, 104:5, Isa. 24:1, Matt. 4:8) ending at four corners (Isa. 11:12, Rev. 7:1) and stretched out over the waters (Ps. 24:2, 136:6). The occurrence of earthquakes, and volcanic upheavals (Ps. 104:32, Amos 1:1, Zech. 14:5) gave the impression that the earthy disc floated on a primitive ocean, and the presence of springs and water at the bottom of wells served to bolster this impression.

While the earth remained relatively still and tranquil

3

(Ps. 18:7, 24:2, 104:5, Eccles. 1:4, Job 38:4, 2 Pet. 3:5, Rev. 6:14), the sun moved (Josh. 10:12,13, Ps. 19:6,7, Eccles. 1:5, Isa. 38:8) in relation to a stationary earth.

When, in the course of time, it became necessary to effect some sort of reconciliation between biblical myth and scientific theory, the ambiguity of portions of the scriptures permitted some degree of harmonization.

First it was pointed out that the Hebrew story of creation is a powerful document, incomparably superior to the creation epics of Chinese, Babylonian, Egyptian and Greek mythologies, which teem with warring gods and monsters.

Remnants of these cosmologies are nevertheless still to be found in the Hebrew Bible. The Babylonian Marduk cleft the water dragon Tiamat in two while fashioning the world. There are also traditions that the Hebrew God Yahweh overcame a monster that either personified or was closely associated with a primeval chaos of waters (Ps. 74:12—15, 89:9,10, 104:5–9, Isa. 51:9,10, Job 26:10–13) but these remnants are submerged in the grand monotheism (Deut. 4:39, 6:4, Ps. 83:18, Isa. 42:8, 43:10, 44:6, 45:22, Zech. 14:9) that made God the sole author of creation. Even though the God of creation is written in the plural number, *Elohim,* and denotes a compound unity, this plurality simply indicates majesty and power.

The 7 days of creation have been elaborated to mean 7 eons of immense magnitude, but probably 24-hour periods were really intended by the biblical editor who referred so simply to ". . . and it was evening, and it was morning . . ." Among the biblical Hebrews (and modern Jews) as well as among some other ancient peoples, the day was reckoned from one sunset to another: the end of the day coincided with the end of the working period. Using this conception we can add a little to Archbishop Ussher's date. The good Bishop should not be criticized for his ignorance of the theory of evolution. He performed an excellent piece of mythologico-historical research. He must be faulted on his theology.

The Bishop was wrong in calculating that God had created the earth on a Sunday morning. He had failed to observe that God began his work the previous evening: "And it was evening, and it was morning, the first day" (Gen. 1:5). He had also overlooked the fact that the Architect of the world did not need to sleep in order to refresh himself and begin work on the morrow, for "Behold, the Keeper of Israel doth not slumber nor sleep" (Ps. 121:4).

The Eternal had no doubt pondered his projected creation for an endless Sabbath. Are we to suppose that the Master of the Universe sat all of Saturday night on his heavenly throne slumbering, or twiddling his divine thumbs? Indeed no, on the basis of Bishop Ussher's calculations, the world must rather have been created on Saturday night, October 22nd, 4,004 B.C.E.

In 530 B.C.E. Pythagoras deduced that the earth was round, and Aristarchus of Samos (250 B.C.E.) suggested that it revolved round the sun. When Galileo proved that it did, it became necessary to find biblical confirmation, and three sentences appeared to serve rather well: Isa. 40:22 refers to "the circle" or "the globe" of the earth while Job 26:7 states that God "hangeth the earth upon nothing." Job 38:14 compares the earth to a pot being turned (on an axis?) before the potter.

The volcanic continents lifted out of the primeval oceans also had their biblical allusion: ". . . the waters stood above the mountains. At thy rebuke they fled . . ." (Ps. 104:6,7).

The emergence of plant life refers initially to grass (Gen. 1:11), possibly microscopic flora. This was followed by herbs, and finally trees.

Animal life is also surprisingly evolutionary in development: first the sea creatures, amphibia, perhaps reptiles, fowl and finally mammals (Gen. 1:20–25). The allusion to whales (*tanin*, Hebrew) might even refer to extinct reptiles like dinosaurs, though a mammalian creature seems more likely if we pay attention to the *tanin* of Lamentations 4:3 "Even the sea monsters draw out the breast, they give suck to their young ones . . ." In other places (Job 7:12, Ps. 148:7, Isa. 27:1) the same *tanin* is called whale as well as dragon.

But that is about as far as we can get in rapprochement. Other difficulties cannot be rationalized and surmounted without straining biblical meaning beyond recognition.

For one thing, there is a different account of the creation story in Genesis 2. The first 3 verses of this chapter rightly belong to the initial chapter. Verse 4 introduces a creation story by a different writer, or at least from a different tradition, together with a slightly different deity who, previously called God, is now called Lord God.

The significance of this observation was first appreciated not by a theologian but by a French physician, Jean Astruc, of Montpellier, round about 1750. In this alternative tale, man is created first (verse 7) out of dust, to be followed by vegetation (verse 9 cf. verse 5), animals (verse 19), also formed from dust, and finally woman (verse 22).

It is disconcerting to observe specific mention of reptiles not on the 5th day, when their appearance is only hinted at, but on the 6th day, after the creation of mammals (Gen. 1:20–25).

One misses the mention of apes prior to the account of the appearance of man. Considering their importance to the theory of evolution, it is theologically disappointing to observe that the first mention of apes is in the Book of Kings (1 Kings 10:22, 2 Chron. 9:21).

The most glaring inconsistency is the matter of the sun.

The Deuteronomist (33:14) recognizes that fruit is brought forth by the sun. So are all plants: can chlorophyll be formed in the absence of sunshine? Yet vegetation flourished before there was a sun to sustain it. The luminaries of heaven were only created on the 4th day (Gen. 1:16).

Bible apologists have generally suggested that the sun was there all along, but mostly shrouded in clouds which finally parted on the 4th day. But this is a flimsy rationalization and certainly not in keeping with the very plain declaration of what took place on the 4th day of creation.

It is tempting to suggest that the biblical editor erred in unwittingly transposing the 3rd and 4th days and that one of the most original versions of the creation epic featured:

1st  day: The creation of all the cosmos, of the uttermost universe (Gen. 1:1, 3).

2nd day: The conglomeration of space particles, eventually to condense into the earth and enter a solar system (Gen. 1:2, 6).

3rd day: Contact with a solar system: appearance of the sun (Gen. 1:16).

4th day: Appearance of plant life (Gen. 1:11).

5th day: Appearance of marine life, amphibia and fowl (Gen. 1:20, 21).

6th day: Further development of reptiles, appearance of mammals, and finally evolution of man (Gen. 1:24–27).

7th day: The world having been set in motion, the Creator desisted from further activity (Gen. 2:2) and left his magnificent works ("And God saw everything that he had made, and, behold, it was very good" Gen. 1:31) to revolve and evolve till the end of time.

This is a much more acceptable interpretation for those who feel that one is needed. Jews in particular can adduce theological support for an evolutionary interpretation of Genesis. The Talmud, a kind of collection of minutes of rabbinical meetings over 1,000 years, teaches the doctrine that the present world was preceded by the creation and destruction of other worlds (Bereshit Rabba 3:7).

However, attempts at harmonization are really idle, for the creation story is not a legend, it has no substrate of truth; it is pure myth, and should be accepted as such.

## Eden

Where was the garden of Eden? The biblical details are as follows:

"And the Lord God planted a garden eastward in Eden; and there he put the man whom he had formed . . . And a river went out of Eden to water the garden; and from thence it was parted, and became into four heads. The name of the first is Pison: that is it which compasseth the whole land of Havilah, where there is gold; And the gold of that land is good: there is bdellium and the onyx stone. And the name of the second river is Gihon: the same is it that compasseth the whole land of Ethiopia. And the name of the third river is Hiddekel: that is it which goeth toward the east of Assyria. And the fourth river is Euphrates" (Gen. 2:8—14).

We can gain no information from the name itself. "Eden" has been identified with a particular district in the Euphrates-Tigris plain, and has also been thought to mean simply "pleasure," "delight," "paradise."

A Hebrew legend places this paradise near the southern Palestine town of Hebron, which served King David as a capital for a short period. Adam was believed to have been created near Hebron and to have died there, though Christian legends suggest Golgotha as his burial place, while Arabs will point out his grave near Mecca.

Generally the garden of Eden has been thought to be in

the Babylonian plain, while the district of Havilah has usually been placed in parts of Arabia or the Yemen.

But there have been other suggestions. In Ceylon there is a mountain called Adam's Peak. The summit has a giant depression rather like a footprint, and Muslims identify it with Adam's foot, though others insist that Buddha was responsible.

Eden has also been placed in Kashmir, Armenia and the Nile delta, while there have also been supporters for Australia, the lost continents of Atlantis and Lemuria, and even the North Pole.

The identification of the rivers of Eden is also difficult. Only the Euphrates is beyond dispute, though a strong case can be made out for identifying the Hiddekel with the Tigris. The Talmud suggests the Gihon as the Nile and the Pison, the first river mentioned, as the Ganges.

But it is possible to maintain quite a different theory, which is dependent not only on considerations of area, of space, but also on the dimension of time.

Current theory holds that man originated somewhere in the south or south-east of Africa. It was perhaps some 2 million years ago that *Homo* parted from the primate stem and left the arboreal life for a terrestrial future. For staggeringly long eons, some 100,000 generations of paleolithic men made their painful way north through warm lands, hunting and foraging for food, until they reached the Middle East; there *Homo* followed the sun through the Fertile Crescent to reach India and China, finally entering Europe and, last of all, America.

By about 30–50,000 years ago Man had sufficient cranial capacity to merit the title of *Homo sapiens*. About 10,000 years ago in the Fertile Crescent of the Near East grain was first sown and reaped by neolithic communities, and this was followed shortly thereafter by the domestication of various animals.

The biblical account lends support:

The name "Adam" means "earth" in Hebrew, but it also means "red" for, significantly, he originated on the red earth—for such it is—of southern Africa. The "garden eastward in Eden" was eastward in Africa.

There was a primeval river entering Eden, not a real channel of water, but the ultimate source, the composite origin of all rivers. Its 4 tributaries watered paradise. The first, Pison, was evidently a major east-sited river in southern Africa, perhaps the Zambesi, and the land of Havilah which it encompasses is none other than southern Africa, where, it is stressed, there is much fine gold and precious gems. Elsewhere (Exod. 28:18, Jer. 17:1, Ezek. 3:9, 28:13, Zech. 7:12) there is reference to "diamonds," an uncertain description, nor is the nature of the precious gems in southern Africa made clear.

Post-deluge references, that is, writings of a later tradition (Gen. 25:18, 1 Sam. 15:7), have attracted the district of Havilah nearer to Canaan, but earlier references suggest otherwise. Havilah (a person) is listed in an African setting as a son of Cush and a grandson of Ham (Gen. 10:6,7, 1 Chron. 1:9). And even though another Havilah is given a Semitic origin (Gen. 10:29, 1 Chron. 1:23) he is manifestly an emigrant to Africa: one of the 13 sons of Joktan (Gen. 10:26ff), this Havilah keeps company with such African sons (districts) as Sheba (Somalia?) and Ophir, which precede him on the east African coast, while the last mentioned, Jobab, evidently reached the tip of Africa.

The term Ophir (Afir) may be etymologically related to Africa. Every three years there were sea journeys from Ophir bringing goods to Solomon's realm (1 Kings 9:26–28, 10:11,22). Two of the products mentioned in many translations, sandalwood and peacocks, have an Indian origin, and are therefore suspect. It seems likely that the former was in fact almug wood, and the latter (mentioned only once in identical passages in 1 Kings 10:22 and 2 Chron. 9:21 and not at all referred to in the New Testament) either chickens or baboons.[1]

The second tributary, the Gihon, has been traceable as the Nile in writings as far back as those of Josephus (1st century) and the Septuagint (Jeremiah 2:18) compiled during the 3rd century B.C.E. Gihon clearly still belongs in Africa, encompassing the land of Cush, rendered in the Authorized Version as "Ethiopia," but probably referring more correctly to Nubia.

The third river, Hiddekel, going "toward the east of Assyria" has been a source of contention. It is generally considered to denote the Tigris. A rather late reference (Dan. 10:4) is quite explicit in this identification, but the early and the only other biblical reference (Gen. 2:14) to the Hiddekel requires a more tortured exegesis to equate it with the Tigris. In Assyrian and Medo-Persic the river's name is Tiger or Tigra, a Semitic corruption of which was known to be Digla, and since the Hebrew *Hai* or *Hi* means "lively," "fresh," and may be coupled with the description of water (Gen. 26:19), the extension to Hiddekel does not strain the imagination.

Yet this exegesis is not so compelling as to preclude other possibilities.

To gather up again the thread of geographical evolution, the next stage of Man's trek north towards Assyria must have encountered the Jordan and the Orontes in the Lebanon-Anti-Lebanon rift, and these composite streams, at a certain stage of Man's geographical development, could be identified with the Hiddekel. Interestingly enough, if the third river is a composite one, Hiddekel is a composite word, the first syllable *Hi* referring to the first river encountered, the Jordan, while *Dekel* denotes the Orontes.

Support for the theory that the Hiddekel is the Jordan-Orontes and not the Tigris is given by a legend that Adam stood for 40 days (i.e. a very long time) within the waters of the Jordan.[2] Moreover, an ancient Babylonian map of the known world at that time ignores the Tigris, and features only the Euphrates, straddled by the city of Babylon.[1]

The garden of Eden was no mythical realm limited to a fabled area in the Middle East. In the primitive and collective memory of Man it lingered as a real habitation originating in south-east Africa and extending over the course of a million or more years up through the geological fault of the east African and Syrian valleys to join the plain between the Euphrates and the Tigris.

Paleolithic Adam spread through the lands of his paradise, hunting and foraging for food (Gen. 1:28,29), and finally becoming a nomad (Gen. 3:23,24) in all the lands, the hot and the cold, of the world.

What color was Adam? Not red, for his name refers to the red earth on which he first laid claim to humanity. As the first human in Africa, he was black. But when he reached the north of Gihon, the Nile, and the rivers of the Fertile Crescent, Adam was brown; in the east, and later in Europe, Adam, still a paleolithic creature, was yellow and he was white. Adam was all colors, and Eve was both blonde and brunette.

What occurred thereafter? How is Adam's wisdom attained toward the end of the paleolithic period? While initially "they were both naked, and were not ashamed" (Gen. 2:25), that is, they were ignorant paleolithic folk, by about 40,000 years ago, Eve saw that the fruit of the tree of knowledge of good and evil was "to be desired to make one wise (so) . . . she took of the fruit thereof, and did eat, and gave also unto her husband with her; and he did eat. And the eyes of them both were opened . . ." (Gen. 3:6,7). Figuratively their eyes were opened, their mental capacities enlarged, and they became *Homo sapiens.*

It should be noted that in Hebrew, pairs of antonyms denote totality, e.g. the "heaven and earth" of Gen. 1:1 really means "everything." Similarly "good and evil" (see also Gen. 24:50, Prov. 15:3, Zeph. 1:12) denote totality. The tree of the knowledge of good and evil was the tree of wisdom, of the knowledge of everything.

Finally, what was the nature of Adam? In the setting of African Genesis, was he timid, or, as has been written, was he a killer, a murderer? The latter view, recently expounded, was severely criticized in anthropological circles. It also disturbed Christian theologians because it interfered with their concept of the Fall of Man from an earlier moral height. And it gets no support from the Genesis myth. Quite the reverse. Adam is depicted as a weak and pusillanimous creature, hiding in fear before the voice of God manifested in natural phenomena (Gen. 3:10). Nor did he lift a finger against himself—his fellow Adams, against his mate or his descendants. His neolithic sons were the first to indulge in fratricide. Adam was a man of peace.

### Adam's Operation

Long before Malthus came on the scene a biblical legend related the tale of how Mother Earth learned that God was about to make a mate for Adam and protested "I have not the strength to feed the herd of Adam's descendants."

One must surely have a stultified imagination to accept that Eve was formed from a miserable piece of bone. The narrative in fact suggests more exciting possibilities. Adam clearly recognized that Eve had in her rather more than just one of his ribs, and what is more important, he referred to the fact that she was flesh of his flesh (Gen. 2:23).

What happened was this: After inducing a general anesthetic the nature of which is quite obscure from the tantalizingly brief account, the Great Surgeon excised the lateral halves of the two lowermost ribs (for use in Eve) on both flanks of Adam. This exposed the underlying adrenal glands, the vital tissue from which Eve was formed. The adrenal is the only andro-gynous organ in the male body and was the obvious choice for fashioning Eve. Unlike all other organs, the adrenal is not curved or rounded but starkly angulated, with sharp edges and flat surfaces, evidence of having been trimmed by a secret scalpel. Adam harbored within him a tissue secreting female hormones; this knowledge permits us to harmonize two alternative and apparently conflicting pronouncements on the creation of man and woman:

"Male and female created he them; and blessed them, and called *their* name Adam . . ." (Gen. 5:2).

"So God created man in his own image, in the image of God created he him, male and female created he them" (Gen. 1:27).

On superficial inspection these declarations suggest that the original being was a bisexual Siamese-twin-like creature. Indeed, archaic legends have held that Eve was tacked onto Adam's back and that God subsequently divided them through their rib-to-rib connection. Such a view, however, receives no support from the observation that "It is not good that man should be alone" (Gen. 2:18). But the inconsistencies vanish when it is postulated that the female body was not stuck to Adam's side, but harbored as a "chemical embryo" within his body. Thus "Male and female created he them . . ." should be understood as "Male and female (in adrenal propensity) created he them . . ."

The warning against eating of the forbidden fruit "for in the day that thou eatest thereof thou shalt surely die" (Gen. 2:17) was in the nature of a postoperative admonition. The biochemical reason for this restriction becomes clear when it is appreciated that the forbidden fruit was neither an apple nor a fig but, as minor legends have suggested, a banana—significantly indigenous to the African setting of the first parents. Bananas contain large quantities of catecholamines such as noradrenaline. Having just completed the most delicate of operations based on a catecholamine-producing organ, the Great Surgeon could well forbid the intake of foods containing pressor amines which might upset the homeostatic mechanisms so recently stabilized. Indeed God subsequently forbade adrenals as an article of diet (Lev. 3:4,15,16).

No surgeon likes to have his orders flouted, so that when the couple ate their fill of bananas God meted out punishment to them both and we have inherited the consequences. Of course, had the silly girl not listened to that snake in the grass in the first place, the world would not be in the present postoperative mess.

A case has also been made out for pomegranates as being the forbidden fruit. Pomegranates have a high content of estrogen (literally "begetter of mad desire"), hence their prominence in the love poem, the Song of Songs.[3]

Despite the translation of the Hebrew *aleh te'enah* as "fig leaf" (Gen. 3:7) it is more likely that Adam and Eve used the larger leaves of the banana plant to make "aprons" for themselves which they suspended from the waist. The term *te'enah* can refer not only to fig but equally well to banana. Biblical and Talmudic Hebrew has no word for banana, a fruit introduced into Palestine only with the Islamic conquest. What word could the Hebrew story teller use to describe a banana leaf, unknown in Israel? The word for fig had to suffice. Sculptors and painters of Adam who have hidden the genitals behind a miserable fig leaf are all in grievous botanical error.

### The Snake in the Grass

Eve has been unjustly branded. The Great Mother was roundly cursed for disregarding the warning of the deity and listening to the wily serpent. And yet, on closer inspection, Eve is seen to be innocent of the crime to which she pleaded guilty.

The serpent has always been considered to be the embodiment of temptation. More than that, he was the personification of the Evil Eye, the malevolent gaze that cast a spell over his hypnotized victims. The gaze of the serpent has been credited with the ability to mesmerize and transfix small birds and animals and to direct the actions of humans. When Eve pleaded that the serpent beguiled her (Gen. 3:13) she was misunderstood by her Judge. The Hebrew term *hishi-ani* goes beyond the implication of simply being misled. It means "hypnotized me," "mesmerized me." Eve had no complete control over her actions. She had diminished responsibility, and had she enjoyed adequate psychiatric and legal representation at the court of Eden, she would have been acquitted.

Eve was thus no weak-willed creature who could not withstand the serpent's urging. It was Adam who was weak-willed, who noted that his spouse came to no harm, and so ate of the forbidden fruit. Legends whisper that a portion of it stuck in his throat, producing the protruberance known as the Adam's Apple. (Of course, it should really be known as Adam's Banana, but such a description is open to misinterpretation.)

### Eve's Punishment

The matter of Eve's sorrow (Gen. 3:16) in labor deserves comment. Though a widespread view is held that Eve was cursed with pain in childbirth, this is an error. The Hebrew *etsev* does not mean pain, but "toil," "labor" (see such usage in Ps. 127:2, Prov. 10:22, 14:23) and excellently describes the nature of parturition. The same word *etsev* is used to describe the punishment accorded to Adam (Gen. 3:17) in deriving sustenance from the earth. ("The Torah," a 1962 redaction of the Masoretic text issued by the Jewish Publication Society of America, renders *etsev* in Gen. 3:16,17 as "pain," "anguish").

Who delivered Eve, and who cut the cord? This is no problem. The couple must have observed the parturition of animals, so that either Eve bit through the cord, or else Adam delivered his wife's infant, cut the cord, and possibly tied it with twine.

### Genetics

Plants (Gen. 1:11) and animals (Gen. 1:21) are given a hereditary pedigree while the first statement on human genetics concerns Adam's third son, Seth: "And Adam lived an hundred and thirty years, and begat a son in his own likeness, after his image" (Gen. 5:3), from which the inference has been drawn that Adam's earlier offspring were not in his own likeness and image. It has been fabled that Adam's first union was with Lilith, a legendary wraith who preceded Eve, and that the offspring of Lilith, like herself, were not quite solid flesh, and were, in fact, the demons who inhabited the Underworld.

But this does not account for the non-Adamic physiognomy of Cain and Abel, which can only be explained on the basis that Cain resembled his mother while Abel did not resemble either parent.

## Adam's Navel

There is a good deal of evidence for regarding Adam as an evolving creature in an evolving world. Not only is there the evidence of his northeastern movements through the garden of Eden, but there is the preceding account of biological evolution in Gen. 1. To clinch matters, Adam gives the game away in Gen. 2:24. Not yet a father, perhaps not yet maritally experienced, he can nevertheless state "Therefore shall a man leave his father and his mother, and shall cleave unto his wife" and this before his eyes were opened in wisdom (Gen. 3:7). Clearly Adam was no orphan, he knew of parents.

But if we disregard the evolutionary evidence and focus our attention on the rest of the legendary account of Adam and his mate, we strike a startling deficiency.

Did Adam and Eve have navels? Not being born of woman, such is not possible. Having had no intra-uterine existence, Adam could have had no navel, no ligamentum teres, and what is more, he could have had no ligamentum arteriosum or foramen ovale. Had the Deity even planned a congenital heart condition for Adam, it could not have been a patent ductus arteriosus or an inter-atrial defect. It is also unlikely that Adam had any appreciable congenital disorder for it is fabled that Adam never fell ill.

Adam could also not have experienced deciduous teeth, and he was probably created a teenager, erupting his third molar only with the attainment of wisdom (Gen. 3:7).

Perhaps it might even have been considered blasphemous to credit Adam with a navel, seeing that he was made in the image of God (Gen. 1:26).

Certainly artists did not take such dilemmas to heart. Michelangelo's Adam in the Sistine Chapel is splendidly umbilicated.

Did Adam possess a navel? Biological Adam, yes; Theological Adam, no.

### Adam's Enzymes

Adam had never been breast fed. Accordingly, on a physiological plane, he needed no digestive ferments to deal with milk sugar. While he required proteases, lipase, amylase, maltase and sucrase (invertase) to deal with the constituents of his adult diet, he had no need for lactase, for he was never a nurseling, and had not yet domesticated animals for their milk. Congenital absence of lactase has been described in babies; this condition might therefore be termed Adam's deficiency.

### Adam's Psyche

Lacking an infancy, were there also psychological repercussions? It seems that Adam was formed as an adolescent. Having noted that all the beasts of the field had mates, whereas he was deficient in this respect (Gen. 2:20), the Lord understood his prurient state, noting that "it is not good that man should be alone" (Gen. 2:18). Sexual feelings in the male are most urgent during adolescence, and this is also the period when the surgeon might want to do an elective major procedure (Gen. 2:21-22): a young adult is unlikely to experience any complications.

Lacking the mishandling of parents, the unconscious

sexually-centered habits of infants, the problems and fears of childhood, puberty and the menarche, the first parents were singularly free of complexes, inhibitions, neuroses and guilt. Only after they were led astray by the serpent (Gen. 3:6) did they develop self-conscious shame (3:7), irrational fears (3:8), hate (3:15), and sorrow (3:16), a legacy still with us today.

## Adam's Fears

For a little eternity Adam lived in the garden of Africa and elsewhere: a precarious life among wild animals, a bitter struggle for survival. Long before he profited from the tree of wisdom, Adamic man struggled from syllable to word, from word to sentence; the better to be able to warn his mate, his children and his fellows of the presence of danger nearby. He wrestled with the elements and survived in a fearsome and capricious world his limited intellect did not permit him to understand.

Paleolithic Adam had much to fear, especially those clans within Adamic man that had not found relatively sheltered peaceful valleys in which to rear their young. It is not to be wondered that Adam should indicate fear when, at dusk, he experiences the manifestations of deity in Nature: "And . . . (Adam) . . . said, I heard thy voice in the garden, and I was afraid, because I was naked; and I hid myself" (Gen. 3:10). The terrifying storms, lightnings, hurricanes, eclipses, gave ample reason for Adam to be afraid and to hide himself.

It is conceivable that this fearful phylogenetic experience of some of the Adamic clans is reflected in the purposeless crying of young infants who are not hungry, not sick, and have no obvious need or discomfort: the so-called "colic". In certain babies, this may be no more than an ontogenetically determined pattern of reaction stamped within the primitive reflexes of the nervous system and indicating the concentrated rehearsal of fear, terror and panic experienced by more than a million years of paleolithic man.

Ask an 8-week-old infant what he feels and he will relate the history of Adam.

Do infants put objects in their mouths because 100,000 generations of Adamic man systematically tested the earth's foods (Gen. 1:29) to discover which were edible and which poisonous?

### Adam's Voice

Adam's reported speech was faultless, but control over vocal function was no easy matter. Coherent speech may have required the passage of a thousand millennia and, while many Adamic clans mastered it in the lower paleolithic, other clans might have experienced a much longer and more painful struggle. Can it be that most stutterers are deficient in cerebral coordination, and that this deficiency might be based on a genetic constitution which can be traced back to paleolithic clans that never completely mastered speech and subsequently lost themselves in marriage with more speech-gifted tribes?

Such defects reappear, as do a number of organic conditions, in apparently sporadic fashion in subsequent generations.

There is some biblical corroboration: Adam's first attempts at speech, the linguistic gropings of lower paleolithic man, are directed, logically and understandably enough, at the identification of animal food and foe, but the stuttering effort is not graphically reproducible (Gen. 2:19–20). Eons later, upper paleolithic Adam finally mastered fluent, nonhesistant reproducible speech (2:23), reflecting not only his coherent use of words, but also his more elevated and advanced sentiments, hundreds of thousands of years removed from mere taxonomy.

While this view of stuttering does not solve any problems—in particular masculine preponderance and the ability to overcome or mask the handicap—it does provide a basis for understanding why stuttering should occur at all among humankind.

### Cain's Allergies

From the time of his birth Adamic man had not tasted cereals, though during the mesolithic era Adam may have been a horticulturist (Gen. 3:23). It could be expected, therefore, that the first individual to eat grain might react unpleasantly to this food which, after all, had been untasted by endless generations of his forebears. Accordingly we can understand the mark set upon Cain (Gen. 4:15), a branding with eczema, an allergic sign, and a symbol of the first ecological misfit.

"And Cain was very wroth" (Gen. 4:5) when his sacrifice was spurned, as a consequence of which ". . . his countenance fell" (4:5), not only figuratively but also literally, manifesting his facially contorted struggle for breath as his latent grain-sensitivity asthma was explosively precipitated by God's rejection.

Despite his allergies, Cain finally met his end through injury. A legendary gloss to Gen. 4:23–24 has his poorsighted great-grandson shoot him with an arrow.

### Cain and Abel: a Reappraisal

Cain and Abel heralded the neolithic era. Anthropologists generally hold that farming preceded animal husbandry, so that Genesis quite rightly lists Cain, the tiller of the ground, as an elder brother to Abel, the keeper of sheep (Gen. 4:2). Since grain farmers were the first to settle into neolithic communities, Gen. 4:17 also correctly notes that Cain built the first city (Cassuto[4] maintains that his son Enoch built it) in the land of Nod, east of Eden (4:16). That too, may be correct, for among the first settled communities of man yet discovered, none are earlier (*c.*8,000 B.C.E.) than at Jarmo in northern Iraq. An equally early agricultural settlement was founded in the southern districts of the Fertile Crescent, at Jericho. This Canaanite portion of Eden in the south Palestine area was identified with a tribe of Cainites (Kenites, Num. 24:22). However, Cain's fabled struggle with Abel has been placed near Damascus[2], possibly an equally early settlement.

From what we know of primitive communities we surmise that the more belligerent were the herders of beasts and cattle, the pastoral folk who from time to time descended from the more arid hill country to devastate the cultivated lands in the river valleys.

With this knowledge we can look with different eyes at what really happened between Cain and Abel. Their struggle was symbolic of real historical events. To reinterpret Gen. 4:3–5, this narrative is not simply a tale of one sacrifice accepted and another rejected. At some period of neolithic culture, and perhaps repeated again and again, natural disasters visited the farmers and the pastoralists of the Fertile Crescent. The grain farmers were especially hard hit by the gods who rejected their sacrifices and supplications and continued to send drought, floods and locusts. The herders of sheep and goats could still manage by moving on to other pastures, but such moves involved the temptation to make use of whatever cultivated fields they might chance upon, and graze their beasts on what little might be left of the crops. It involved enmity and battle with the settled agriculturists for possession of their lands.

And so Abel attacked Cain, and Cain killed his brother in self-defense and in defense of his farms, his homes, his women and children.

The Bible narrative supports this thesis. Consider Gen. 4:8: "And Cain talked with Abel his brother: and it came to pass, when they were in the field, that Cain rose up against Abel his brother, and slew him."

Students of Hebrew can appreciate the misleading translation in the Authorized Version phrase "And Cain talked with Abel his brother . . ." The Hebrew *vayomer* is only rarely used in the context of "talked with" (2 Chron. 2:1), and even in these instances one is not certain that the content of speech is not missing. Almost invariably the word means "said" and is followed by what was said. In the context the Hebrew reads "And Cain said unto Abel his brother: and it came to pass . . ." This speech was no conversation between a gentle unsuspecting Abel and a psychopathic, insanely jealous, murder-planning Cain. Cain had something to tell Abel. And what did he say to Abel? Clearly a verse is missing, no doubt deliberately omitted or suppressed by the Genesis story teller, understandably perhaps, considering the widespread biblical preferance for the pastoral life.

Both the Septuagint and the Samaritan Pentateuch as well as other ancient readings supply a tame addition: "And Cain said unto Abel his brother: let us go into the field; and it came to pass . . ." Such additions reflect not a common original reading but a common inference based on the continuation of the verse.[4]

The 1962 Jewish Publication Society of America rendition of the Masoretic text shows commendable honesty in leaving out the unknown verse: "And Cain said to his

brother Abel . . . and when they were in the field . . ."
We can easily guess the missing line: "And Cain said unto
Abel his brother: keep off my fields; and it came to pass . . ."
Interestingly enough a biblical legend [2] supports this thesis.
It is fabled that the brothers' quarrel began as a result of one
of Abel's sheep wandering onto the fields of Cain, who was
angry to find it grazing there.

In current usage, the angry farmers warned the pastoralists: "Keep your sheep off our property; don't trespass; we
barely have sufficient for our own needs; we will not tolerate
invaders; enter our fields at your peril."

Yet we read that "and it came to pass, when they were
in the field . . ." Whose field? Cain's field! What was Abel
doing on Cain's property? Abel was the symbol of the herders of sheep who attacked the folk and the fields of the river
valleys. Cain retaliated and drove off the enemy.

Cain was no murderer. The Hebrew term used for his
slaying is *harag* (killing, manslaughter or murder) and not
*ratsakh* (murder) the word employed in the sixth commandment, which should read "Thou shalt not murder." Nowhere is Cain called a *rotseakh*, a murderer.

In apportioning blame, the Bible demonstrates its usual
favoritism for the youngest son and overlooks Abel, the cov-
etous aggressor, and condemns the innocent retaliation of
Cain. Indeed a biblical rumor unwittingly supports the suggestion that Abel, the herder, was the aggressor. He is fabled
to have been physically stronger than Cain, and well capable
of assaulting his elder brother, but Cain won the struggle as
a result of a ruse and slew the attacker.[2] If not the biblical
editor, then at least the Deity recognized Cain's crime as
manslaughter rather than murder and did not impose the
stern sentence of a life for a life. Indeed Cain's punishment
(Gen. 4:12–14) was identical to that already inherited from
Adam (Gen. 3:17–19,24) as a consequence of his disobedi-

ence. Not only did Cain get an oblique discharge, but he was even granted a protective device (4:15).

Subsequent generations of Jews (Matt. 23:35) continued to regard Abel as the innocent one, as did also Christians: "Cain, who was of that wicked one, and slew his brother. And wherefore slew he him? Because his own works were evil, and his brother's righteous" (1 John 3:12). But this is all wrong. Abel was a greedy, angry, sinful man and this knowledge permits us to offer a daring exegesis for a perplexing passage in Genesis, perhaps one of the most difficult in the Bible. Disappointed by his God or gods who had blighted his crops while an aggressive Abel hovered nearby, Cain is understandably depressed (Gen. 4:1): "And the Lord said unto Cain, why art thou wrath? and why is thy countenance fallen? If thou doest well, shall thou not be accepted? and if thou doest not well, sin lieth at the door. And unto thee shall be his desire, and thou shalt rule over him" (4:6,7).

This translation obscures the difficulties of the Hebrew which, at first glance, appears to be corrupt. Cassuto[4] translates as follows: "Surely, if you do well, you will be upstanding; but if you do not do well, sin shall be a *rovetz* at your door; its desire shall be for you, but you will be able to master it." Cassuto[4] comments: "In modern times the expositors have found the text so hard to elucidate that some, like Gunkel and Jacob, have actually abandoned all hope of understanding it and have left part of it untranslated."

The Septuagint rendering is even more obscure than the Hebrew and the 1962 Jewish Publication Society translation, basing itself on the knowledge that the *rovetz* was a kind of Babylonian demon, renders the crucial passage thus:

> Surely if you do right  (Hebrew verse obscure)
> There is uplift
> But if you do not do right

Sin is the demon (*rovetz*) at the door
Whose urge is toward you
Yet you can be his master.

Without exception, exegetes have seen in this comment some sort of theological homily while Christians have been eager to find in it evidence of original sin and the universality of guilt.

But this seems very odd; how can it be that in the midst of a dramatic struggle between agriculturist and pastoralist, a curious piece of theology on sin is suddenly and unaccountably interposed and is then promptly ignored and forgotten as the drama unfolds? Surely the passage must have a more immediate relevance to the epic struggle?

A crucial clue is provided by one of the very difficulties in the most obscure line of all concerning sin lying or crouching at the door. The word that all exegetes translate as "sin" is the Hebrew *khatot* and it is feminine gender (masculine: *khet*). This *khatot* is crouching (*rovetz*) menacingly towards Cain who, somehow, will be able to master it. The term for crouching, *rovetz,* which qualifies the feminine *khatot* is written in the masculine gender (feminine: *rovetzet*). How is it that a *khatot* is in the process of *rovetz?* This is very curious Hebrew.

*Khatot,* however, can also mean a sin offering, a sacrifice (*khet* cannot have this meaning) and in this context it is often used with reference to male animals, e.g., Exod. 29:36, Lev. 4:3, Num. 7:87, 2 Chron. 29:21, Ezra 8:35, Ezek. 43:19,21,22. In the context of the Cain-Abel struggle, *khatot* is not theological sin at all, it is Abel himself, who must expiate his sin and become a sacrifice, hence it is Abel who crouches (*rovetz*) to menace Cain, and the masculine gender is correct.

The very name Abel (*Hevel*) suggests his evil role. The

27

word is commonly translated "vanity" but it has a connotation of sinfulness and is often coupled with other iniquitous attitudes. The presence of *hevel* may be sufficient to arouse anger in God (Deut. 32:21) and this wicked *hevel* ("vanity," Authorized Version) which provokes God to anger is coupled with the people's sins (*khata'ot*) in a single sentence (1 Kings 16:13,26).

Accordingly, the obscure passage in Genesis can be understood within the context of the drama. The righteous Cain has been let down by his God; perhaps his God was testing his faith? Abel waits without. The situation is fraught with danger. The sense of the obscure passage is then not a rebuke to a sinner but encouragement and comfort to a trusting soul. Cain's God says in effect:

> Surely if your trust is true
> You will rise (from your depression)
> But if your trust is not true
> At your door the *khatot* (Abel) crouches
> To menace you.
> Yet you can overpower him (as I promise you by
>     my hint that Abel will be his own *khatot*).

And Cain, trusting in God, proceeds to do just that with Abel, who acts as his own sin offering, his own expiation. The view of Abel as a sin offering gains further credence from the subsequent allusion to Abel's blood being spilled on the ground (4:10,11), the blood being an essential element in an expiatory offering.

No sooner is Abel dead however than God, for the first time, adopts what at first glance appears to be a moral stance: excusing or ignoring his own plan for Abel, God deplores Cain's act; no more than that however; there is no outrage, God simply chides Cain in terms which are surprisingly similar to those previously uttered to Adam for eating a forbidden fruit:

| | |
|---|---|
| And the Lord God called unto Adam, and said unto him, Where art thou? (3:9) | And the Lord said unto Cain, (in hiding?) Where is Abel thy brother? (4:9) |
| And he said . . . I was afraid . . . and I hid myself (3:10) | And (Cain) said, I know not: Am I my brother's keeper? (4:9) |
| And (God) said . . . Hast thou eaten of the tree . . . ? (3:11) | And (God) said, What hast thou done? (4:10) |
| And unto Adam he said, Because thou hast . . . eaten of the tree . . . cursed is the ground for thy sake . . . Thorns also and thistles shall it bring forth to thee (3:17, 18) | And now art thou cursed from the earth . . . When thou tillest the ground, it shall not henceforth yield unto thee her strength (4:11, 12) |

The Abel of Cain is thus somehow equated with the fruit of Adam, and the violation of Abel is no more reprehensible than the eating of the forbidden fruit. Abel is a taboo, the fruit is a taboo, the peculiar property of God and not to be violated by man.

Having established that the natures of Cain and Abel are the exact opposite of what they are usually considered to be, it is possible to expand a little on their genetic dispositions.

It has already been noted that only Seth was made in the image of his father (Gen. 5:3) and, indeed, it says that Adam begat Seth (5:3). Concerning Cain it says nothing of the sort and his mother claims that she got him from God (4:1), and a biblical legend [5] recounts that Cain had an angelic face quite unlike that of his father; presumably he resembled his mother, while Abel, the criminal, resembled neither. Of him it is not stated that Adam begat him or that God was thanked for Abel's birth; he simply arrived (2:1). Did he grow up unwanted and rejected?

On the other hand it has lately been shown[6] that many tall criminals and persons with anti-social tendencies have a curious genetic make-up, often possessing an extra Y chromosome, so that whereas normal males have an X sex chromosome derived from the mother and a Y sex chromosome derived from the father and thus have 46-chromosomed cells designated XY, criminals often have the 47-chromosomed cell structure labelled XYY. Perhaps Cain and Seth had the expected XY and Abel the unhappy XYY.

The nature of that chromosomal maverick, Abel, permits us to speculate further on the subject of the original sin which is responsible for the hereditary taint which Christians see in man.

There are many views on the nature of original sin, some not even related to Adam. The lust of divine beings for mortal women (Gen. 6:1-4) is held to have generated demon progeny responsible for worldwide corruption. There are legends that these demons were also spawned by Adam's first spouse, the wraith Lilith. Freud reasoned that since Christ, a type of Adam (Rom. 5:12-19, 1 Cor. 15:21,22,45-49) sacrificed himself, his suicidal penance could only mean that the original Adam, the Son, had made an attempt (successful?) on the life of the Father, God. Original sin was thus attempted murder, if not deicide.

The general Christian view, however, is that the essence of the Fall is Adam's disobedience, if not revolt, against God. But this seems a very superficial and trifling explanation. The commandment which he disobeyed, the prohibition of the forbidden fruit, was not the first given to Adam. In the variant of the Genesis story as related in Chapter 2, the first understanding, if not instruction, was that Adam was to take care of Eden, and we are not told that Adam defied God in this particular.

Furthermore, it was not Adam who initiated the program of disobedience; it was Eve, and how could she be blamed when she was not given this commandment by God? It was only told to Adam (2:17) at a time when Eve had not yet been created. She learned of it only by inference from the serpent (3:1) or from Adam (3:2,3). And Adam's was not a willful disobedience but more in the nature of ignoring of a prohibition which evidently caused no harm to Eve, notwithstanding the dire threats of death (2:17). In eating, Adam in fact demonstrated a commendable loyalty to his spouse (3:17). His action could hardly be described as disobedience, much less revolt against God. At most it was a minor and thoughtless indiscretion.

Is original sin original sex? There is much to recommend this view. Adam's trifling disobedience led to momentous consequences: an awareness of sexuality. No sooner had God forbidden the fruit (2:17) than he said "It is not good that man should be alone" (2:18). Clearly the prohibition was related to Adam's connection with a projected mate. And no sooner had they eaten of the fruit and become aware of sexuality (3:7) than God was aroused to explore their act (3:8,9) and question them first on sexuality (3:11) and thereafter on the fruit (3:11).

The Satan-Serpent had introduced the first couple to sex, the bait and the promise of immortality not in person (3:22) but in progeny; this too rendered him akin to the gods (3:5,22) and, if man was to be reconciled to his immortal Maker, he had to demonstrate his own mortality, his own finiteness, to his Maker. In this context Christ's (i.e. Adam's) Golgothic suicide also makes sense, for in this manner he propitiates God, he gives a practical demonstration that, in human garb, man is mortal after all. Of course Adam had suffered the dissolution of old age (5:5), but it could do much to placate and convince God of man's continuing finiteness if a subsequent Adamic equivalent would lend emphasis to this feature by dying, not from old age or disease, but by publicly demonstrating that man's mortal body was destructible. The spirit might be resurrected, but dust returned to dust.

Paul's recurrent attacks on sex lend cogency to the view that, for Christians, original sin is original sex. Niebuhr[7] writes of original sin as "an inherited corruption, the precise nature of which could significantly never be found by theologians, but which they most frequently identified with the sexual lust." Kaufmann[8] concurs: "sexual desire appears here as the archetypal sin" and this view gets an echo in the cry of David "I was shapen in iniquity; and in sin did my mother conceive me" (Ps. 51:5).

If the concept of original sin producing a hereditary corruption is repellent on a moral plane, it has validity at a genetic level. The blemish associated with sex only blighted one of Adam's three sons, Cain and Seth being free of chromosomal defects. Thus it is not sex *per se* which constitutes original sin but the occasional sexual union which brings forth a chromosomal anomaly, the possession of which may disrupt the orderly functioning of society. Original sin operates not at a coital but at a chromosomal level. The proper study of theology must therefore include teratology, physical and behavioral, for "The wicked are estranged from the womb: they go astray as soon as they be born" (Ps. 58:3).

The nature of the mark of Cain has excited little curiosity but 3 factors permit us to make a fairly accurate diagnosis:

1. It was a long-standing or even permanent affection.
2. It was an eczema, as has already been clarified, and eczema is notoriously chronic.
3. It was red. Cain's mark is called, in Hebrew, *ot*. This word means a sign, a token, and it is used many times in the Hebrew Bible but on four occasions it signifies, in addition, the presence of color:

   a) It appears in the rainbow, a token of God's covenant with Noah (Gen. 9:12,13,17).
   b) It is a token of the covenant of circumcision (Gen. 17:11).
   c) It is a protective device derived from the blood of lambs which has been smeared on the doorposts of the Israelites in Egypt (Exod. 12:13,23).
   d) It is the token, the scarlet cord, used by Rahab (Josh. 2:12,18).

Where was the mark and what was its shape? Some legends may be mentioned if only to dismiss them at once as having little or no support: It has been written that the mark was in the shape of the Hebrew letter *tet* tattooed on his arm, or that the mark was on his brow and took the form of the Hebrew letter *heh* (the chief letter in, and a common abbreviation for the Hebrew word meaning God), or else looked like a tree or a horn.

A valuable clue is provided by the purpose of the mark. It was a protective device designed to ensure continued life for Cain (Gen. 4:15). Moreover, it was not a token of contempt, a mark of a murderer, for Cain was no murderer. It was a sign on one who had found God's favor either because he had repented of his deed or because he had not been guilty of murder anyway. Accordingly Cain qualifies as a righteous man and we know from a passage in Ezek. 9:4,6

*33*

that righteous men in Jerusalem, whose lives were also to be preserved, had a mark placed on their foreheads.

So Cain's mark was on his forehead. The Jerusalemites, we are told, were marked with the letter *Tav,* which means a sign, and this is the only occasion in the Hebrew Bible when the letter *Tav* is used alone.

There is good reason to suppose that the eczematous patch on Cain's brow looked like the Hebrew letter *Tav.* In ancient Hebrew, as in Phoenician, Greek and Egyptian hieroglyphic, the letter *Tav* (or *Tau*) took the form of a cross. The cross is a universal symbol, long predating Christianity. The handle of the cross, the top section of the vertical bar, tends to vary a lot. It may be equal in length to the other three arms (the Greek cross) or may be a good deal shorter (the Latin cross), may be expanded into an oval ring (the Egyptian *ankh* or *crux ansata*), or may be absent altogether, then looking like the Greek *Tau* or the English capital letter T, which again features in mythology as the hammer of Thor and which survives to this day as the gavel of the chairman.

The cross was known in Sumeria some 4,000 years B.C.E. It was revered in Babylonia and Anu, the chief of the Babylonian gods, had a cross for his symbol. A large cross amulet is suspended from the neck of King Tiglat Pileser, as may be seen in the Nimrod Tablet at the British Museum. In Egypt the *crux ansata* was known as the sign of life and victory over death.

During the early 1900's a Semitic scholar, Robert Eisler, found and photographed a clan of nomads in Arabia who carried a red mark, a cross, tattooed on their foreheads.

It is suggested that the mark of Cain was an eczematous red patch on Cain's forehead, rather in the shape of what has now become known as the Christian cross.

That Cain was more sinned against than sinning was well appreciated by one of the flurry of gnostic and heretical sects that arose during the era of Christ. In the second century, a sect calling themselves the Cainites espoused the cause of Cain, and undertook to defend as well the reputation of other reprobate biblical characters such as Esau and Judas, by no means unmitigated blackguards, as they are usually misrepresented.

Strangely enough, no biblical commentators have appreciated the anthropological nature of the conflict between Cain and Abel as interpreted here. Of course lots of anthropologists and mythologists understand that there is here a conflict between agriculturists and pastoralists but do not see the interpretation as presented here. Cassuto's exegesis[4] is labored and unconvincing.

### Patriarchal Longevity and the Flood

The story of Adam is only completed with the death of Noah. There are 10 generations from Adam to Noah and the secret of their longevity is to be found in the opening verse of Chapter 5: "This is the book of the generations of Adam," a sentence which, in the Hebrew, can also be read "This is the book of the generations within Adam" or ". . . generations comprising Adam." Like Adam, the names of the other mighty men of old are merely concentrations of, or representations of numbers of generations, hence their lifespans of close to 1,000 years. With Noah the prehistoric period ended and the lifespan was limited to a reasonable 120 years (Gen. 6:3).

After an abortive attempt to draw a Cainite genealogy (Gen. 4:17–24) for Noah, a more seemly ancestor, Seth, is invented (Gen. 4:25, 5:3) and a suspiciously similar lineage is established to link Noah to Seth.

From the birth of Seth to the Flood, in Noah's 600th year (Gen. 7:6), was 1,526 years, so that if Seth was born at

*35*

the beginning of the neolithic period in the Fertile Crescent (8–7,000 B.C.E.), then the Deluge inundated widespread portions of the Middle East round about 6,000 B.C.E.

With the advent of written records about 3,000 B.C.E., the Sumerians in the lower Euphrates-Tigris valley were already repeating marvellous tales of a Great Flood, differing versions of which were related by the Semites who succeeded them.

The Biblical account of the Flood is a little difficult to believe. Especially incredible is the statement that the waters covered every mountain under heaven (Gen. 7:19), that every living organism upon earth perished (7:20–22) and that chosen pairs of all "that creepeth upon the earth" (7:8–9) were induced to enter the Ark.

It is a pretty tale but not for literal consumption. What probably happened is that some perspicacious or visionary farmer on the banks of the Euphrates some 6,000 years B.C.E. lashed a few logs together and made a covered raft, reasoning that the next time the river flooded its banks to dangerous proportions, or the next time a massive downpour threatened, the raft would serve him handsomely.

And the Flood came, so he bundled his family and personal belongings onto the raft, together with a few goats and sheep, a tame bird and maybe one or two other pets, and set sail, hoping to escape the watery wrath of the gods.

Probably he survived the local deluge, and with the passing of each century the tale was embellished until the Flood encompassed the whole earth, and Noah repopulated it.

### Noah the Comforter

Lamech called his son Noah, saying "This same shall comfort us concerning our work and toil of our hands, because of the ground which the Lord hath cursed" (Gen. 5:29). His grandfather Methuselah, knowing the role for which Noah was destined, and hoping to save him from the influence of the Evil Eye in the interim, suppressed his real name and called him Menachem instead.[2]

Both Noah and Menachem are derived from the same Hebrew root meaning to comfort.

The riddle is: In what way was Noah a comforter? Instead of an explanation, or a narration of a fulfilled prophecy, there follows an account of the Flood.

The biblical editor reverts to the original theme after concluding the account of the Flood. In Chapter 9 he makes it clear why Noah was a comforter, and the reason for his name is seen to be very appropriate:

"And Noah began to be an husbandman, and he planted a vineyard. And he drank of the wine and was drunken . . ." (Gen. 9:20,21).

Alcohol is a superb tranquilizer and comforter: "Give strong drink unto him that is ready to perish, and wine unto those that be of heavy hearts. Let him drink, and forget his poverty, and remember his misery no more" (Prov. 31:6,7); "wine that maketh glad the heart of man" (Ps. 104:15).

### Noah, an Albino

Under the title of "Noah, an Albino," Sorsby[9] makes use of extracts from the pseudoepigraphical Book of Enoch (1st century B.C.E.?), from a Dead Sea Scroll fragment (1st century B.C.E.?) and from the apocryphal Book of Jubilees (4:28) to prove that Noah was an albino.

From the first book we learn that "Methuselah took a wife for his son Lamech, and she bore him a man child. The body of the babe was as white as snow and red as a blooming rose, and the hair of his head and his long locks were as

*37*

white as wool, and his eyes like the rays of the sun. When he opened his eyes he lighted up the whole house, like the sun . . ." [2]

Little wonder that he was chosen for a great endeavor.

Sorsby concludes that both Lamech and his wife Betenos were recessive carriers of the gene for albinism and, because they were first cousins, the original carriers must have been not Methuselah or his spouse but Enoch or his wife. There his speculation ends.

But his argument in favor of Enoch can be taken further. Among the recital of the generations issuing from Adam, only Enoch is credited with a relationship to God; indeed, he did not even die but was simply taken up to heaven (Gen. 5:24).

In this angelic realm of innocence, white, a symbol of purity, would not be out of place. Enoch, with a special affinity to heaven, clearly derived his whiteness therefrom, and was the first man to bring this heavenly feature to earth. Albinism is a heavenly trait, a reminder from the gods, handed down by Enoch to Noah, the first albino.

If Noah was the first, was Samson another? He had an unusual name: little sun, while the lady who extinguished him was Delilah (night), surely an ex-post-facto invention. This play on words, light versus darkness, does not mean, as so many commentators have thought, that the Samson story is a solar myth. There was good reason for him to be called "little sun." His barren mother had already despaired of having a child, so consider her exultation when she bore him. He was the light of her life, her little sunshine. But there were other names to call an adored son, why a manifestly solar name? Can it be that he had yellow hair, like the rays of the sun, that he was an albino? There was certainly something very special about his hair as the secret of his immense strength. It is pure conjecture, of course; but if hair is especially noteworthy, so much so that it is compared with the sun's rays, then albinism is at least a possibility.

## REFERENCES

1. Kraeling, E. G. (1956): *Bible Atlas.* Rand McNally, New York
2. Ginsberg, L. (1956): *Legends of the Bible.* Simon & Schuster, New York
3. Bigg, S. (1967): *Journal of the American Medical Association,* 199: 343
4. Cassuto, U. (1961): *A Commentary on the Book of Genesis.* Transl. I. Abrahams. Hebrew University Magnes Press, Jerusalem
5. Graves, R. and Patai, R. (1964): *Hebrew Myths, the Book of Genesis.* Cassell, London
6. a. Casey, M. D. *et al.* (1966): *Lancet,* 2:859
   b. Price, W. H. and Whatmore, P. B. (1967): *British Medical Journal,* 1: 533
   c. Annotation (1967): *British Medical Journal,* 1: 64
7. Niebuhr, R. (1956): *An Interpretation of Christian Ethics.* Meridian Books, New York
8. Kaufmann, Y. (1961): *The Religion of Israel.* Transl. M. Greenberg. Allen & Unwin, London
9. Sorsby, A. (1958): *British Medical Journal,* 1: 1587

# THE PHYSICIAN AND DISEASE

Abraham brought with him no medical lore from his native Babylonia. His performance of circumcision was foreign to the physicians of Ur and Haran. Moses too, left behind him the medical legacy of Egypt and preached instead an austere medicine emanating from the Godhead. A medical deity was not new to the Egyptians of course. The great Thoth was a healing deity, while Imhotep—priest, magician, architect and statesman as well as physician—had been elevated to godhood. Joseph in Egypt had employed "physicians" (Gen. 50:2) though it is possible that they limited their practice to embalming. To the east, the Babylonians had a practical knowledge of drugs and herbs including the opiate laudanum, while the Code of Hammurabi (1700 B.C.E.) laid down rules for medical practice.

## God the Physician

What was new, as god-physicians go, was the exclusiveness of the Yahweh of Moses. A jealous God, his monopoly of healing left no room for such as the magician-physicians of Egypt and Babylonia.

"I am the Lord your physician" (Exod. 15:26). "I kill and I make alive," declared Yahweh, "I wound and I heal"

(Deut. 32:39). God is credited with taking sickness away (Exod. 23:25), and as late as the period of King David (1000 B.C.E.) God was credited with healing all diseases (Ps. 103:3). "O Lord heal me, for my bones are vexed" (Ps. 6:2). "I cried unto thee, and Thou dids't heal me" (Ps. 30:2). "Who hath made man's mouth? or who hath made the dumb, or deaf? or the seeing, or the blind? have not I the Lord?" (Exod. 4:11).

God acted by divine fiat, he declared his curative edicts, needing no intermediary charms, spells, magicians or physicians. His word alone was effective. His word had created the cosmos (Gen. 1). In the beginning was the word (John 1:1). "So shall my word be that goeth forth out of my mouth: it shall not return unto me void, but it shall accomplish that which I please . . ." (Isa. 55.11). "He sent his word, and healed them." (Ps. 107:20)

In the Covenant of Abraham and in the Law of Moses, God's medical role was so unique that it left no room for any to participate in or to detract from his medical prowess.

During the early formative years of Israel's history, orthodox medical practice was probably limited to the care of surgical injuries, while the Egyptian remnants of magico-medical practitioners must have had a hard time of it contending with Moses' legislation against wizardry, sorcery and the like.

But Moses himself practised medicine, and good medicine at that, though his role as a physician has been overlooked, partly because of his immense stature in other fields as a leader of men, and partly because of the all-pervasive medical influence of his God.

Moses, as well as modern experts on preventive medicine, would hardly have agreed with the opinion of Christ (Mark 2:17) that "They that be whole need not a physician, but they that are sick." Moses legislated on food habits, personal habits and sexual hygiene; he introduced a weekly day of rest, population registration, measures for the detection, prevention and seclusion of contagious illness, and appointed public health officials—the most important being Aaron, his brother. Aaron's office, however, was a priestly one, indicating the investment of medicine in religious garb, in contrast to its magical investments outside of Israel.

It does not detract the slightest from Moses' remarkable contributions to the preservation of health to mention that the Assyrians also had food taboos, regarding the pig as unclean, i.e. ritually, not hygienically unclean. Conceivably the pig, the wild boar, was the totem animal—hence sacred—of some Semitic tribes. The Chaldees considered "leprosy" to be infectious and banished the afflicted from the community. The Babylonians believed that certain days of the month (among others, the 7th, 14th, 21st and 28th) were "unlucky" and unproductive, so that no work was done on them.

Moses also wielded the physician's emblem: the serpent upon a staff (Num. 21:8–9), and this before the time of Aesculapius. The serpent and staff of Moses was so effective in halting an obscure epidemic (Num. 21:6) in the wilderness that, long after the death of Moses, it remained as an object of idolatry (2 Kings 18:4).

### Emergence of the Physician

The influence of Moses and the God of Sinai was incompatible with the presence of physicians among mortals, but some hundreds of years after Moses' death, about 1200 B.C.E., his influence had waned considerably. Indeed, by 700 B.C.E. Isaiah, who wrote the first 39 chapters of the collection under his name, found no cause to invoke the name of Moses; nor did Amos, about 750 B.C.E.

There is a legend that Hebrew Medicine began with

King Solomon, who was the author of all medical knowledge and wrote a Book of Remedies which was later suppressed by King Hezekiah. Hebrew physicians are first encountered some 300 years after the death of Moses. At this time, about 900 B.C.E., Solomon's kingdom had already split in two—a southern Judah and a northern Israel—later dispersed as the Ten Lost Tribes.

With the accession in 913 B.C.E. of King Asa of Judah, the physician came into his own. Asa was the son of Rehoboam and the grandson of Solomon. In 1 Kings 15:8 Asa is erroneously stated to be the son of Abijam, but Verses 2 and 10 make it clear that he and Abijam were in fact born of the same mother. The brother's name is incorrectly called Abijah in 2 Chron. 12:16ff. The Chronicler preferred Jah (Hebrew God) to Jam (Canaanite sea god), for he could not countenance an idolatrous name in the Davidic House; but the older Kings tradition is correct.

Abijam ruled for 2 years (was he very old at death?), to be followed by his younger brother Asa, who must have ascended the throne at a mature age. He reigned for 40 years, so that he was well-advanced in age when he became "diseased in his feet" (2 Chron. 16:12). Since the illness lasted 2 years (16:12,13), presumably he had arteriosclerotic disease, perhaps gangrene, or less likely, gout.

The Chronicler notes, however, that in his illness Asa "sought not to the Lord" (for shame!) "but to the physicians." In the opinion of the Chronicler, Asa had shown lack of faith in God's priests; clearly he deplored Asa's consultation with the lay physicians, an action especially reprehensible in one who had spent his energies in the cause of Yahweh, removing pagan images, hounding illegitimate priests and destroying Canaanite cults. Not wholly successful, Asa had overlooked, among other objects, the idolatrous golden staff and serpent of Moses—which was finally smashed by the virtuous Hezekiah (2 Kings 18:4) about 700 B.C.E.

But as king, Asa had blazed a trail. Though he died (2 Chron. 16:13) following the ministrations of his physicians, he showed the path, and qualifies for the status of a famous patient.

Thereafter it must have been a good deal easier for physicians to make headway, though their work was still duplicated by priests and prophets.

Elijah (about 870 B.C.E.) dabbled in medicine. He revived a child (artificial respiration?) with respiratory difficulty—possibly asthmatic, more probably infective or due to an inhaled foreign body (1 Kings 17:17–22).

His successor Elisha (about 850 B.C.E.) may properly be described as a general practitioner. By means of mouth-to-mouth breathing (2 Kings 4:34) he revived a 3-year-old boy with heat stroke. In passing it may be noted that the boy was not taken to Elisha's office; the physician-prophet made a house call (2 Kings 4:32). He transferred "leprosy" from one person to another (5:27), made poisoned food edible (4:40,41), smote a hostile company with blindness (6:18,20), evidently battled unsuccessfully against an embarrassing baldness (2:23), disinfected a water supply, or alternatively, understood something of fluid and electrolyte balance (2:21), was the obvious person to be consulted by an ailing foreign king (8:8) and, though aware of the fatal prognosis, was sufficiently compassionate to withhold such knowledge from the patient, thus contributing to resolving a modern ethical dilemma: "Go say unto him, Thou mayest certainly recover; howbeit the Lord hath shown me that he shall surely die" (8:10).

Rabbinic commentary has commended Elisha's words as befitting a physician, but has condemned Isaiah's brutal attitude to Hezekiah when the king was "sick unto death": "Set thine house in order; for thou shalt die, and not live"

(2 Kings 20:1). Though prophetically in order, such words were not worthy of a physician. The Hebrew term for physician, *rofeh*, is derived from a root meaning to ease, to assuage, and the traditional Jewish attitude has always been that a patient should never be told that the end is near.[1]

Compassion for the sick is strikingly manifest in Hebrew semantics. Displaying a remarkable insight into the essence of compassion, the Hebrews drew on the word *rehem*, womb, to epitomize the essence of *rahamim*, compassion. It is akin to the feelings a mother has for her offspring: "Can a mother forget her sucking child, that she should not have compassion on the son of her womb?" (Isa. 49:15). What is required in a physician is not a heart of stone but a heart of flesh (Ezek. 11:19).

The dying might be spared suffering by dulling their senses with merciful wine (Prov. 31:6,7, Ps. 104:15) and at a postbiblical date it was customary to ease the death of those sentenced to judicial execution by drugging them first with wine and myrrh (Talmud, San. 43a, 45a, Semahot 2:8).

The sick also required the comfort derived from compassionate visitors (Sira 7:35) and God himself had set an example as a comforter for the sick, for so the rabbis (Sotah 14a) have interpreted God's visit to a recently circumcised and ailing Abraham recuperating by the oaks of Mamre (Gen. 18:1).

## The Physician Established

Parallel with the medical practice of the priests and prophets, orthodox medical practice, partially released from Mosaic restrictions, proceeded apace. When King Joram, at the time of Elisha, was wounded in battle with the Syrians, he withdrew to Jezreel in order to receive medical attention (2 Kings 8:29, 9:15). Some 200 years after Asa's example, Hezekiah, also a God-fearing ruler, suffered no opprobrium when he became ill and resorted to medicaments rather than to prayer (Isa. 38:21). Isaiah (about 700 B.C.E.) referred to ointments (1:6) and to (surgical) healers (3:7), and 100 years later Jeremiah considered health and healing (30:13, 33:6, 46:11, 51:8) and wondered at the lack of physicians and medicaments in Gilead (8:22).

Ezekiel, a younger contemporary of Jeremiah, wrote (47:12) of the use of leaves for medicinal purposes. Such herbal remedies are also noted in Rev. 22:2. The author of Proverbs (17:22) understands that "A merry heart doeth good like a medicine."

Luke (10:34) mentions the antiseptic properties of alcohol, and a Pauline writer (1 Tim. 5:23) comments on the medicinal virtues of wine.

Medicinal baths must have been popular, especially the hot springs of Tiberias and the pool of Bethesda in Jerusalem (John 5:2).

By the 4th century B.C.E. physicians were certainly well established, and Job refers familiarly and contemptuously to "physicians of no value" (Job 13:4). Somewhat later Tobit, who had diseased eyes, "went to physicians but they could not help me" (Tob. 2:10). Because priests in Jerusalem's sanctuary, by virtue of their contact with carcasses, were especially prone to enteritis, they required the services of physicians attached to the temple.[2] With the burgeoning of rabbinical commentaries at this time, support for physicians was even found in the law of Moses: a man who injured another "shall cause him to be thoroughly healed" (Exod. 21:19), from which the inference was drawn that a physician was sanctioned to administer a healing agency (Berahot 60a). Indeed the 1962 Jewish Publication Society translation renders the passage "he must pay for . . . his cure" and the ancient Septuagint: "shall pay for . . . the expense of his cure." Josephus, commenting on this passage, also makes a note about paying the physician (Antiquities, IV, 8:33).

Shortly after 200 B.C.E. ben Sira manages to praise the physician while at the same time explaining his relationship to the Supreme Physician: "Honour a physician according to thy need for him, for verily the Lord hath created him" (38:1).

He also observes that "a long illness baffles the physician" (10:10), a point illustrated by Luke's account of "a young woman having an issue of blood twelve years, which had spent all her living upon physicians, neither could be healed of any" (Luke 8:43).

Luke, widely accepted as a dear and glorious physician, requires more extended consideration. His case history of Christ is disappointing. Like the three other evangelists, he presents a picture of a serene wraith mouthing arcane thoughts in ethereal settings. Though his Greek is good, and though he added some very helpful biographical details, the case history he presents, and his interpretation thereof, can only leave a modern physician perplexed and dissatisfied. The symptoms and signs are incredible, the setting obscure and inchoate, the examination of the subject uncritical and lost in a fog of mystery and ambiguity. The diagnosis is contradictory and naive. In an age which saw doctors like Soranus and Galen, it is disappointing to observe how careless and credulous Luke reveals himself to be.

But then Luke was no physician, and nor was he a traveling companion to Paul. Both these commonly held assumptions are fiction.

There are a number of Marys in the New Testament just as there are a number of Judases, Marks and others. There is even more than one Jesus (Acts 7:45, Heb. 4:8, Col.

4:11, Matt. 27:17 in ancient Caesarian text; see New English Bible). There are also a number of Lukes but this is no reason for supposing that they are the same individual.

During his imprisonment in Rome (60?–64 c.e.) Paul knew a "beloved physician" called Luke (Col. 4:14), and during this period he also wrote of Luke (here not characterized as a physician) in 2 Tim. 4:11 and Philem. 24.

Now Paul was a very sincere and truthful witness, even when it came to relating such matters as his hallucinations. When he mentions that Luke was a beloved physician, we may be sure that he was indeed.

However, the difficulty is that not all the writings under the name of Paul are from the pen of Paul. It is generally accepted among competent theologians that some of Paul's letters are spurious, and these include Colossians and Timothy (Philemon is probably genuine). Nevertheless they may contain truthful historical kernels and Luke the physician may well be among them.

What connection does this physician have with Luke the evangelist, the one who wrote the third gospel and the Acts of the Apostles? Well, they share the same name, and that is the sum total of evidence.

A further link has been sought by trying to show that Luke the evangelist writes like a physician (how does a physician write?), but this is an impossible and unproductive quest. All that can be shown is that Luke's vocabulary is much more extensive than that of the other evangelists and that he writes far better Greek. "At one time it was claimed" writes Professor Caird [3] "that the use of medical terms in these books was striking enough to prove that their author was a doctor. It has since been shown that the same argument would have made doctors of almost all the writers of antiquity, and that the whole thesis is in any case ill-founded, since Galen himself claimed not to use a medical jargon but to write in the common parlance of ordinary men." Professor Grant [4] concurs, adding that, if anything, Luke the evangelist must have been a veterinarian.

What is significant is that nowhere in his writings does Luke the evangelist ever state or even hint that he was a physician, or that he ever treated a patient, let alone cared for a sick and injured Paul, in his alleged journeys with him.

As for Luke the evangelist's alleged journeys in the company of Paul, this fiction was first suggested as fact by Irenaeus near the end of the 2nd century and about 100 years after Luke's writings appeared. Origen, in the 3rd century, suggested that Luke the evangelist was none other than the Lucius (Luke) of Rom. 16:21; and a similar synthesis between Luke the evangelist and the Lucius of Acts 13:1 was suggested by Ephraim Syrus of the 4th century.

Luke the evangelist is commonly thought to have accompanied Paul because in four passages (Acts 16:8–17, 20:5–15, 21:1–18, 27:1–28:16) he suddenly and unaccountably writes about "we." This first person plural has taxed the dialectic of theologians for centuries. It is impossible that these "we" passages refer to Luke the evangelist. They are either copied, as many theologians consider, from a "travel diary" of a companion of Paul or else represent a corruption by later editors of Luke's work: "the text of Luke has been subject to a good deal of modification." [4] "The 'we' passages are not the eye-witness report they pretend to be; they are a literary device to give the narrative greater vividness and verisimilitude." [5]

Among lesser reasons, Luke the evangelist could not have been a companion of Paul because:

1) Nowhere in Acts does Luke mention even a single conversation that he might have had with Paul. Nowhere is

there real evidence of personal intimacy or familiarity with Paul. "In Acts we have no photograph of Paul taken by a colleague." [4]

2) Luke largely ignores the specific Pauline teachings as revealed in his major epistles.

3) Instead of Paul, Luke relies heavily on Mark for his record, repeating virtually half of Mark's gospel.

4) In many places Luke's account of Paul's travels is in irreconcilable conflict with Paul's own versions.

5) Paul was imprisoned about 57 C.E. from which time he was effectively removed from the missionary scene. One would imagine that if Luke had been his companion that he would have written his gospel and Acts at about this time or very shortly thereafter. In fact Luke's writings date from about 90 C.E. (the devout claim as early as 75 C.E. and the sceptics as late as 120 C.E.). It seems incredible that a fervent companion of Paul should wait 30–40 years before putting his jottings together. In fact, Luke the evangelist and Paul the apostle belong to different generations. The truth of the matter is that Luke never met Paul.

Just as Paul, John, Mark, Matthew and Luke (I think their writings appeared in this historical order) had never seen Jesus in the flesh (it is not generally known that the gospels are not eye-witness accounts), and wrote only from hearsay, so Luke too wrote of Paul only from hearsay.

Of Paul the apostle and of Luke the evangelist we know a good deal, but of Luke the physician we know nothing. Exit Doctor Luke.

Though physicians were well established in New Testament times (Matt. 9:12, Mark 5:26, Luke 4:23), and Christ wrought some mighty cures, the role of God's surrogates in healing had by no means lapsed: "Is any sick among you? Let him call for the elders of the church; and let them pray over him" (James 5:14).

This dichotomy in healing has continued unchanged to the present. Two thousand years ago ben Sira could write "My son, when you are sick . . . pray to the Lord, and he will heal you . . . There is a time when success lies in the hands of physicians, for they too will pray to the Lord that he should grant them success in diagnosis and in healing" (38:9,13,14).

Diagnostic methods must have embraced the faculties of seeing, hearing, touching and smelling. There is no better description of these methods of diagnosis than in the moving story of how Isaac was deceived by Jacob:

"And it came to pass, that when Isaac was old, and his eyes were dim, so that he could not see . . . And Jacob said to Rebekah his mother, Behold, Esau my brother is a hairy man, and I am a smooth man: My father peradventure will feel me . . . And Isaac said unto Jacob, Come near, I pray thee, that I may feel thee . . . and he felt him, and said, The voice is the voice of Jacob, but the hands are the hands of Esau . . . and he smelled the smell of his raiment . . . and said . . . the smell of my son is as the smell of a field" (Gen. 27:1–27).

Smelling is often noted, including the odor of wounds (Ps. 38:5) and of the ointments of apothecaries (Eccles. 10:1). Of particular interest is the smell associated with the children of Ammon (2 Sam. 10:6). Throughout the ancient Middle East were dotted temples of Ammon. Frequented by camel-traveling devotees, these temples were early noted by the Greeks to be associated with the pungent smell of decaying camel dung; this smell seeming to belong to Ammon, hence the Greek term Ammonia.

As for more modern methods of diagnosis, visions of auscultation and stethoscopes are surely conjured up by auditory observations like "my bowels shall sound like an harp" (Isa. 16:11), a fairly good description of borborygmi, while

Jeremiah (48:36) knew something akin to cardiac murmurs: "mine heart shall sound like pipes." (Heart transplants are mentioned in Ezek. 11:19, 18:31, 36:26). Lungs are not mentioned in the Bible.

Returning again to dichotomy in diagnosis and treatment, it should be noted that today the position is little different. If anything, the extent of paramedical practice is greater, embracing not only Godly influences, but other transcendental, mystical and magical influences too numerous to mention.

Currently, "Births" entries in newspapers commonly report a "happy event" by noting "Next to God, thanks to doctor and staff."

It is revealing to enter the foyer of the Michael Reese Hospital in Chicago and see engraved on its walls the Hebrew lettering for "Who is like unto Thee, O God!"

## Disease

A parallelism exists between the evolution of the physician in Israel and the development of concepts of disease. In a theocentric society where God could proclaim an uncompromising "I kill and I make alive; I wound and I heal," there was clearly little place for disease-producing intermediaries between God and man.

With the passage of time, however, the immediacy of God's role in illness receded a little into the background, permitting the appearance of non-Godly intermediaries as causes of illness, while God remained the ultimate cause of disease and of its cure. A thousand years after Moses' God spoke in Deuteronomy, his role in medicine was again recorded, but with a slight change of emphasis. About 150 B.C.E. ben Sira (38:2) wrote "Healing comes from the Most

High," an opinion which is easily interpreted to mean that in the final analysis, it is God who heals. About 50 B.C.E. the author of the apocryphal "Wisdom of Solomon" (16:12) wrote "For neither herb nor poultice cured them, but it was thy word, O Lord, which heals all men." Clearly the ultimate credit for cure did not belong to the herb or poultice itself.

During this millennium a factor has progressively interposed itself between man and God. This factor is an agent of disease and a means for its eradication. With the increasing importance of the intermediary factor, the physician too became more important, though the ultimate credit for cure was neither with the physician nor his herbs and poultices; it was God's word.

In the period when God alone killed and cured, the cause of disease was clearly God's anger. There is little question but that a goodly portion of illness was considered to be consequent on a visitation of God's wrath as a result of sins committed by earlier generations. "God layeth up his iniquity for his children," pronounced Job (21:19). The author of Lamentations cries (5:7) "Our fathers have sinned . . . and we have borne their iniquities." And Leviticus (26:29) states "they . . . shall pine away in . . . the iniquities of their fathers."

Passersby, noting a man with congenital blindness, asked of Christ whether this was due to his parents' sin, or to his own transgression (John 9:2). This is an odd query, for if born blind, his sin must have occurred *in utero* (or in a previous life?). In any event Christ denied that either had sinned (9:3).

King David sinned, and as a result "The Lord struck the child . . . and it was very sick" (2 Sam. 12:15). A widow's son fell ill "And she said unto Elijah, what have I to do with thee, O thou man of God? art thou come unto me to call my sin to remembrance and to slay my son?" (1 Kings 17:18).

This attitude to sickness as being caused by sin was never fully obliterated (indeed, it still exists today) so that even in New Testament times we find sin responsible for illness: "Behold thou art made whole: sin no more, lest some worse thing happen to thee" (John 5:14).

Disease, or at the very least misfortune, as a consequence of earlier sin is embodied in the Decalogue: "I the Lord thy God am a jealous God, visiting the iniquity of the fathers upon the children unto the third and fourth generation" (Exod. 20:5).

From a medical point of view this pronouncement presents a difficulty: One would have expected allusions to inherited disease only after the 7th commandment (adultery) rather than after one dealing with idolatry. On the other hand, the idolatry of the Canaanites was commonly associated with religious prostitution, so that inherited disease in this context becomes understandable.

The Hebrews were told the penalty for transgression of the Law: among various catastrophes enumerated, it was also written that the Lord would "appoint over you terror, consumption, and the burning ague (Lev. 26:16) . . . I will also send wild beasts among you which shall rob you of your children (26:22) . . . I will send a faintness into their hearts . . . and the sound of a shaken leaf shall chase them, and they shall flee, as fleeing from a sword; and they shall fall when none pursueth (26:36) . . . The Lord shall make the pestilence cleave to thee (Deut. 28:21) . . . (and) . . . shall smite thee with a consumption, and with a fever, and with an inflammation (28:22) . . . (and) . . . with the boil of Egypt, and . . . emerods, and with the scab, and with the

54

itch (28:27) . . . The Lord shall smite thee with madness, and blindness, and astonishment of heart" (28:28).

If they repented of their sins and were righteous, God promised that he "will take sickness away" (Exod. 23:25) and that he would "put none of these diseases upon thee . . . for I am the Lord that healeth thee" (15:26). Moses is convinced, for he pleads to the Lord on behalf of his leprous sister "Heal her now, O God, I beseech thee" (Num. 12:13). Isaiah gives all therapeutic honor to God: "the Lord bindeth up the breech of his people, and healeth the stroke of their wound" (30:26), and the Psalmist sings (147:3, 103:3) "(the Lord) healeth the broken in heart, and bindeth up their wounds . . . (the Lord) healeth all thy diseases."

Israel was conceived of as the Suffering Servant of God and is especially well portrayed in the famous 53rd chapter of Isaiah. In Verses 3 and 10 it is stated that (Israel) suffered from *holi*, disease. Understandably, Christian translators, unable to conceive of a diseased Christ, render this word as "grief" (e.g. in the Revised Version). But *holi* can never mean grief; it can only mean disease. The diseased Servant of God is Israel, as is made clear in other portions of Deutero-Isaiah (41:9, 42:1,19, 43:10, 44:1,2,21, 45:4, 48:20, 49:3,-5,6). Isaiah pictures Israel as "crushed with disease" (53:10) and Primo-Isaiah elaborates on the nature of this affliction (1:5,6). At one time Jeremiah considered Israel's illness incurable (30:12).

However, within a few hundred years of the death of Moses, God's wrath (i.e. sickness) as a consequence of sin was questioned most eloquently in the Book of Job (6th–3rd century B.C.E?). Here this theocentric argument is splendidly repudiated, and God himself cannot supply a satisfying answer to the presence of undeserved sickness and evil. Instead he dwarfs Job's pitiful yet spirited queries with majestic poetry and cosmic obfuscation.

By the time that Asa's physicians were ministering to him, sickness was no longer always occasioned by sin, and God's role in illness was no longer exclusive. Other agencies had been invoked, and these maleficent intermediaries increase in importance with the approach of the New Testament period. With God's role in illness rather more remote, more pressing agents—especially demons—are incriminated as the immediate causes of illness.

## Micro-Demons

Long before Israel appeared on the historical scene, demons had been accepted as a cause of illness—especially in Babylonia and Assyria, but also in Egypt. Despite their preoccupation with their wonderfully interesting pantheon of gods, the Egyptians evidently also feared evil spirits, if we may judge from the incantation of one anxious mother:

"Run out, thou who comest in darkness, who enterest in stealth . . . Comest thou to kiss this child? I will not let thee kiss him . . . Comest thou to take him away? I will not let thee take him away from me. I have made his protection against thee out of efet-herb, which makes pain; out of onions, which harm thee; out of honey, which is sweet to the living and bitter to the dead; out of the evil parts of the ebdu fish; out of the backbone of the perch." [6]

The Egyptian demons were often messengers of Sekhmet (literally "The Powerful"), the leonine-headed goddess wife of Ptah. She brought pestilence and death to those who neglected her. But she who knew how to kill also knew how to heal, and the Priests of Sekhmet formed one of the oldest associations of doctors and veterinary surgeons. The invocation of Osiris also helped to battle the demons of Sekhmet.

The Babylonians and the Persians had a particularly well-systematized demonology, which penetrated Hebrew thought especially during the 500 years following their Babylonian exile. Prior to this period demons played little part in the causation of illness. Even where they did, such as the evil spirit of Shechem (Judg. 9:23) or the evil spirit that troubled Saul (1 Sam. 16:14), they were sent by God himself. This direction from God is really no great advance in thought; for the Babylonian demons, like the Egyptian emissaries of Sekhmet, while largely autonomous, also only afflicted people when the wrathful gods delivered the sinners into the hands of the demons, or else did not extend protection against the spirits.

The devils ("goat demons" Jewish Publication Society of America, 1962) of Lev. 17:7 and Deut. 32:17 are probably demons whose power and autonomy had elevated them to the station of idols and gods. Their small part in the causation of illness gradually increased in significance so that the New Testament fairly bristles with demons, devils and unclean spirits (Mark 1:21–28, 5:1–20, Matt. 8:28–34, Luke 4:33–36, 8:2,26–39, Acts 19:12–16) and with the largely neurological disorders they were imagined to occasion (Mark 2:5, 7:25–30, 9:17–27, Matt. 8:6,13, 9:2, 12:10,13, 15:22, 17:14–18, Luke 5:17–26, 6:6,10, 7:2,10, John 5:2–14, Acts 3:2, 9:32–35, 14:8).

The Talmud, parts of which are contemporaneous with the New Testament, also has portions devoted to demonology, and the Talmudic form of exorcism sounds rather more impressive, certainly more vituperative (and effective?), than simply expelling them in the name of Jesus: "Be split, be accursed, broken and banished, son of mud, son of an unclean one, son of clay, like Shamaz, Merigaz and Ishtemaah" (Shab. 67a).

In the 5th century Augustine could write: "All diseases of Christians are to be ascribed to demons . . . they torment . . . even the guiltless newborn infants."

If we substitute "germs" for demons, then his opinion is almost modern, and it makes especially good sense if taken in conjunction with the story related in Mark 5. Having exorcised a demon from a man, Christ asked the demon its name. Such full identification was mandatory in order to completely overcome it. The demon replied "My name is Legion: for we are many" (5:9).

Such an admission of profusion, together with the necessity for accurate identification, illustrates an uncommonly penetrating prognostication, for the whole field of bacteriology and virology is foreshadowed.

One particular demon, Lilith, seemed to specialize in afflicting children, and to a lesser extent, men. She was a well-known Assyrian demon who occasionally materialized in the form of a beautiful woman, and then set about molesting men and children. She is specifically mentioned in Isaiah 34:14 by the Hebrew term *lilith,* which is usually translated as "night monster" or "screech owl." Lilith is also commonly considered to be the "terror by night" of Psalm 91:5, but this is a misrepresentation consequent on the confusion of "Lilith" with the Hebrew term *lailah* (night). In fact, "Lilith" is related to Sumerian terms for "wind" (*lilu:* masc., *lilitu:* fem.) .[7] In this respect, wind and gusts of air become demoniac agents of disease.

Hebrew legend supplies two hypotheses on the origin of demons. They were thought to have been the offspring of Adam and the phantom Lilith, while another fable relates that on the 6th day of creation, just after God had fashioned man, He turned to create an even higher order of being, but had hardly managed to construct their souls when the hastening Sabbath obliged him to desist from his labors. Thus it is that these frustrated spirits, demons, have no bodies.

Parturient Mesopotamian women wore charms and

amulets and chanted incantations in order to protect their offspring from the demon Lilith, who loved to suck the blood of infants. Especially prone to molestation were newborn babies, but Zoroaster, at his birth, laughed aloud, and the surrounding demons scattered in tumult and terror. In the idyllic period prior to the flood, newborn infants had no difficulty in waging a successful battle against the demons who sought to molest them. It is possible that the very term "lullaby" (*lili aby*) originally denoted an incantation against Lilith. In later years among the Hebrews it was believed that the eve prior to the day of circumcision was especially hazardous for the infant, for on that night Lilith was wont to play her most foul tricks. In order to forestall her, the parents and well-wishers stayed up the whole night and spent it in feasting and studying the Bible and Talmud.

The demons that the Underworld spewed forth customarily hunted in groups of three, and one infamous Babylonian triad sported the female demon Lamastu (earlier rendition: Labartu), who also specialized in the pediatric field. The administration of a foul medication was a favorite method of exorcising them from the body. It is interesting that the Christian conception of the devil is similar to the Mesopotamian representation of some of their demons, and medieval and renaissance painters pictured him in very much the same manner as did the Assyrian artists.

Both Hebrew and Christian demonologies are derived from the primitive superstitions of their eastern neighbors, and in particular, from the demonology, magic and dualism of the Persians, who overran the Near East while the Hebrews were in exile in Babylonia. The Persian religious influence at that time was that of Zoroaster (about 600 B.C.E.) who preached a religious dualism of a constant struggle between Good (manifest by the divine person Ahuramazda) and

Evil (exemplified by the spirit Ahriman). It is this selfsame Ahriman that was later inherited by the Jews and Christians as Satan, though this widely accepted supposition is by no means proven or accepted by all scholars.

The pre-exilic Isaiah clearly accepts the demon Lilith (34:14), but Deutero-Isaiah evidently rejects her as well as Persian dualism in favor of Yahweh (45:6,7): "I am the Lord and there is none else. I form the light, and create darkness: I make peace, and create evil: I the Lord do all these things."

## Heavenly Bodies

Gods and demons do not exhaust the field of primitive pathology. The astrologers knew only too well that an eclipse foreboded evil tidings. The stars, the sun and the moon exerted their influence also on the health of man. The Psalmist promised (121:6) "the sun shall not smite thee by day, nor the moon by night." The moon, of course, was none other than the great Egyptian god Thoth who has restored the health and the sight of the child-God Horus. It is not surprising that the heathen of Canaan burned incense "to the sun, and to the moon, and to the planets, and to all the host of heaven" (2 Kings 23:5).

Ezekiel complains (8:16) about the sun worshipers, while Malachi (4:2) credits the sun with healing.

In the air were also gusts of wind, which facilitated the air-borne spread of disease (Exod. 9:8,9): "And the Lord said . . . Take to you handfuls of ashes . . . and . . . sprinkle it toward the heaven . . . And it shall become small dust in the land of Egypt, and it shall be a boil breaking forth . . . upon man, and . . . beast."

Even the water on the earth could be a source of illness: "Thus saith the Lord, I have healed these waters; there shall not be from thence any more death" (2 Kings 2:21).

## The Evil Eye

Bewitchment, sorcery and magic—proscribed by Moses—were potent causes of illness. They were most likely to be manifest in the form of the Evil Eye, to which there are some references in the Bible as also to the potentially injurious effects of eyes (Prov. 23:6, 28:22, Matt. 6:23, 20:15, Mark 7:22, Luke 11:34).

Isaiah (13:17,18) thunders "Behold I will stir up the Medes against them . . . and they shall have no pity on the fruit of the womb; their eye shall not spare children."

Ezekiel orders (9:5) ". . . smite; let not your eye spare."

The healed Eye of Horus has been depicted in charms called *udjat* and was invoked among the Egyptians, if not among their Hebrew slaves. *Udjats* were illustrated in an ocular fashion and this selfsame sign, the Eye of Horus, is still invoked, in slightly altered fashion, ℞, to head a doctor's prescription.

The pharmacopoeia of the biblical physician was fairly extensive.[8]

Olive oil was in plentiful supply and was used as an emollient both in health and disease. It was used as a dressing for hair and skin and was applied to bruised or ulcerated areas (Luke 10:34, James 5:14). A sick Herod was bathed in warm oil (Josephus, Ant. XVII, 6:5, War, 1, 33:5).

Several plants were thought to have medicinal properties, especially pomegranates (Num. 13:23, 20:5). It is a measure of their worth to observe that they featured on temple decorations (1 Kings 7:20, Jer. 52:22). With numerous seeds, pomegranates symbolized fertility, and had a sanctity which made them, or those eating of them, immune to demonic influences. In the Middle East infusions of pomegranate

61

blossoms were used for flatulence in infants. In Egypt pomegranate rind was used as a fumigant and anthelmintic. The juice of the pulped fruit (Song of Sol. 8:2) made a refreshing drink in feverish conditions.

Wormwood (Deut. 29:18, Prov. 5:4, Jer. 23:15, Lam. 3:15,19, Amos 6:12), a bitter substance related to absinthe, was used as an infusion for worms and fever. Cassia (Exod. 30:24, Ezek. 27:19) also had general medicinal value.

The bitter and poisonous gall, or hemlock (Deut. 29:18, 32:32, Job 20:16, Ps. 69:21, Jer. 8:14, 9:15, Hos. 10:4) is thought by some to refer to the bitter seeds of the poppy plant.

Another narcotic is the mandrake (Gen. 30:14, 7:13), related to the plant *Atropa belladonna.* The "baaras" plant mentioned by Josephus (War, VII, 6:3) is clearly the mandrake which, he claims, is employed by sick people to nullify demonic influences. In Assyria the root of the mandrake was used to prepare anodynes; and Dioscorides, an army surgeon in the service of Nero, was reputed to have used mandrake wine as an anesthetic.[8]

Several herbs were used for stomach disorders, as carminatives or for sweetening the breath (Song of Sol. 7:8?). Cummin (Isa. 28:25,27, Matt. 23:23) was employed by the ancients as a carminative and condiment and is still used in making curry powder.

Mint (Matt. 23:23, Luke 11:42) was popular in the Middle East as a carminative and ingredient for enemas but there is some doubt whether mint was grown in Palestine during the biblical period.

Anise (Matt. 23:23) was more probably the related herb dill, a carminative and still listed in current pharmacopoeias. Its seeds were chewed to sweeten the breath.

Coriander (Exod. 16:31, Num. 11:7), a carminative, is also used today. So is fennel ("fitches," Isa. 28:25,27).

Many aromatic resins were employed (some also used in the temple cultus) as deodorants, fumigants and perfumes. Myrrh (Ps. 48:8, Prov. 7:17, Song of Sol. 3:6, 4:14, Esther 2:12. Note that Gen. 37:25, 43:11 are mistranslations and do not refer to myrrh) was used for perfuming the body (and corpses, John 19:39), clothing and bedding, and was also employed as a salve for ulcers, as eye ointments, mouthwash and constituent of enemas.

Aloes are also deodorants (Num. 24:6. The "aloes" of Ps. 45:8, Prov. 7:17, Song of Sol. 4:14 probably refer to a different plant, ? eaglewood) and so are hyssop (Lev. 14:6,49, Num. 19:6, Ps. 51:7, Heb. 9:19), myrtle (Neh. 8:15, Isa. 41:19, 55:13), frankincense (Lev. 6:15, Isa. 60:6, Jer. 6:20, 48:35, Ezek. 8:11) and balm (Gen. 37:25, 43:11, Jer. 8:22, 46:11, 51:8, Ezek. 27:17)—all of which were used for local application.

The tares (Matt. 13:25) resembling wheat or rye were weeds known as the darnel plant, and bread contaminated with too much darnel was thought to occasion nausea, convulsions and blindness.[8]

### REFERENCES

1. Jakobovits, I. (1959): *Jewish Medical Ethics,* Philosophical Library, New York
2. Corswant, W. (1960): *A Dictionary of Life in Bible Times.* Transl. A. Heathcote. Hodder & Stoughton, London
3. Caird, G. B. (1963): *Saint Luke: The Pelican Gospel Commentaries.* Penguin Books, London
4. Grant, R. M. (1963): *A Historical Introduction to the New Testament.* Collins, London
5. Sandmel, S. (1958): *The Genius of Paul.* Farrar, Straus & Cudahy, New York

6. Durant, W. (1954): *The Story of Civilization: Our Oriental Heritage.* Simon & Schuster, New York
7. van Selms, A., Professor of Semitic Languages at the University of Pretoria. (1959): Personal communication
8. Harrison, R. H. (1966): *Healing Herbs of the Bible.* E. J. Brill, Leiden

# BACTERIOLOGY

Biblical bacteriology is no remote subject. It sometimes has surprising relevance to the present: for example, Medical Officers of Health are concerned with problems of quarantine for various illnesses. This subject assumed critical importance in 14th century Italy when the country was ravaged by repeated epidemics. It was observed that whereas Gentiles perished in great numbers, Jews escaped lightly. This phenomenon was explained as being a consequence of Jewish laws on cleanliness and of ritual washing after handling dead bodies or associating with impurities. Based upon some rules in Lev. 12–15, Jews generally observed a 40-day period of ritual cleansing, abstention and isolation; and this biblically based custom was made compulsory for the Gentiles as a means of containing the epidemics. The Italian word for 40 is *quaranta,* hence quarantine.

As for notification of serious contagious illness, medieval Jews blew the *shofar*—the ram's horn—after the identification of the third instance within a community, and in the case of diphtheria, with the first patient.

ben Sira (18:19–21) foresees, condones and even encourages measures (immunization?) to prevent disease. It can be inferred from Jer. 21:9 that he who flees a pestilence in the city may be expected to live but that he who remains in the city will die.

### Sanitary Prophylaxis

The biblical Hebrews were fanatical about purity and cleanliness, perhaps because they were intended to be a nation of priests. In this respect they probably borrowed to some extent from the Egyptians among whom they had lived for many years. Egyptian priests as well frequently washed their bodies and clothes, and drank only boiled or filtered water of whose purity they were inordinately proud. They drank from cups of bronze which they cleaned out daily. They inspected meat prior to its sale or consumption. They even possessed primitive flush toilets.

Whatever they might have owed to the Egyptians, the Israelites were obsessed with cleanliness; for them it was in truth next to Godliness: the camps of Jacob and the dwelling places of Israel had to be fit as habitations for their God. Before eating Jews washed their hands (Mark 7:3). They also washed "cups . . . pots, brased vessels, and . . . tables" (Mark 7:4). To this day orthodox Jews ritually wash their hands before meals, reciting the prescribed blessing in Hebrew: "Blessed art thou, O Lord, our God, King of the Universe, who has sanctified us with His commandments, and instructed us concerning the washing of the hands."

Such liberal use of water among a desert people is especially remarkable. There were even occasions when water was so scarce that it was sold (Isa. 55:1). The necessity for ceremonial cleanliness resulted in places of worship and synagogues being built near a river bank.

The Hebrews made soap from nitre (Hebrew: *neter*) or lye (sodium carbonate), ubiquitous in the Middle East. Either nitre, with its sodium content, or the ash of various plants with their potassium content, was heated with olive oil to make soap (Jer. 2:22. For action of acetic acid on alkali, see Prov. 25:20).

Not only was body and clothing to be clean, and the water pure, but meat, which tends to rapid spoilage in a hot climate, was rigidly controlled. The meat of an animal found dead was forbidden (Lev. 17:15, Deut. 14:21, Exod. 22:31, Ezek. 4:14). Even meat found in the house of a dead person was unclean (Num. 19:14) and contaminated meat had to be burned (Lev. 7:19). According to tradition, any blemish such as lung disease or dense pleural adhesions rendered a carcass unfit for consumption. Flesh had to be eaten on the day of slaughter, though in some cases could be left until the second day, but on the third day had to be burned (Deut. 16:4, Lev. 7:15–17, 19:6). Contaminated feeding utensils were required to be destroyed (Lev. 11:33).

The Hebrews burned their refuse outside their camp, and buried their feces (Deut. 23:12–14). Corpses were promptly buried, though it is possible that in rare instances of pestilence they were also cremated (Amos 6:10). It is tempting to draw the inference that fire was used (Num. 31:21–24) in order to sterilize captured enemy materials. If so, this was simply incidental; no doubt its primary purpose was ritual rather than hygienic, for objects which could not withstand fire were also to be washed in the water of lustration (Num. 19:1–10, 31:23) consisting of a suspension of the ashes of a totally burned red heifer, a mixture hardly recommended as an antiseptic. Nevertheless the Hebrews were familiar with primitive antiseptics like oil and wine for dressing wounds (Luke 10:34). Spitting was forbidden (Lev. 15:8, Num. 12:14) as leading to uncleanliness. They forbade tattooing (Lev. 19:28) with its attendant risk of needle-transmitted hepatitis. Jaundice is probably meant by the *yerakon* of Deut. 28:28, for this Hebrew word means green. The Revised Version and the 1962 Jewish Publication Society of America translation render it "mildew," a noncommittal term. In other places (1 Kings 8:37, 2 Chron. 6:28, Amos 4:9, Hag. 2:17) *yerakon* refers to a yellow-green fungus infection of plants.

An orthographic error in the Masoretic text enables one to correct a theory on the role of flies as carriers of disease. Ahaziah, king of Israel, having suffered a serious accident, sent messengers to the Philistine city of Ekron to consult Baalzebub (2 Kings 1:2,3). This name means "Lord of Flies." It has been suggested that the ancients might have noticed a relationship between the swarming of flies and the development of epidemics and they may have deduced that the flies were forms of demon causing the illness. Unhappily, the theory lacks any support other than semantic because the god of Ekron was not Baalzebub as written but Baalzebul (Exalted), an Ugaritic deity whose name has been found on shards from excavations at Ras Shamra. Zebul became corrupted to Zebub (l and b are very similar in Hebrew) but his role as an exalted god may still be discerned in the New Testament references to Beelzebub, not a fly-god but the prince of the demonic gods (Matt. 10:25, 12:24,27, Mark 3:22, Luke 11:15,18).

Our admiration for the Bible's hygienic provisions should be tempered by the understanding that for the most part the purpose of the Mosaic laws was not medical but ritual. Sanitary advantages were hardly more than incidental by-products: "Because thou hast made the Lord . . . thy habitation, There shall no . . . plague come nigh thy dwelling" (Ps. 91:9,10). Possibly the greatest of all ritual as well as hygienic provisions was the introduction of a weekly day of rest. Perhaps one should not stress too much the cleavage between ritual and hygiene. This is a modern separation. In a culture featuring priest physicians, ritual and hygiene are not divorced. An attentive reading of Chapters 13–15 of Leviticus, for example, or Chapter 19 of Numbers, reveals an intense interest in health and hygiene, ritual notwithstanding. Not only is there an interest in the health of persons but even in the cleanliness and safety of surroundings. Houses had to be built with ramparts so that one could not injure oneself by falling from the roof (Deut. 22:8).

A complaint that "It seemeth to me there is as it were a plague in the house" (Lev. 14:35) was sufficient to bring a priest with his purificatory measures. In purifying the house, as in purifying those with "leprosy, scall, rising, scab and bright spot" (Lev. 14:54–56) use was made of the shrub hyssop (Lev. 14:49,54), which King Solomon noticed growing on walls (1 Kings 4:33). In the purificatory ritual of Num. 19, involving the red heifer, hyssop is also used (19:18) and David, after sinning against Uriah and Bathsheba, pleads to be cleansed from sin by means of hyssop (Ps. 51:7).

It is of interest to learn that the penicillin-producing fungus, *Penicillium notatum,* was first identified in 1911 by the Swede R. Westling; he found it growing on a hyssop plant. Pliny (Nat. Hist. 20:15) claimed that pulverized hyssop leaves used as a dusting powder were effective in cutaneous eruptions and inflammations.

Prohibitions against the eating of blood (Gen. 9:4, Lev. 3:17, 7:26,27, 17:12–14, 19:26, Deut. 12:16,23–25, 15:23, 1 Sam. 14:32–34) and, in some circumstances, fat (Lev. 3:16,17, 7:23–25) are observances of long established taboos, the blood and fat being sacred to God.

Some animals were forbidden as food because they were "unclean." This description has no relation to bacteriological or hygienic states; ritual uncleanliness is quite different. Indeed the animals were taboo because they were sacred to numbers of Semitic tribes over centuries and millennia. The pig was not forbidden for health reasons. Its common infestation with tapeworm and trichina is irrelevant. In any event trichinosis probably dates from medieval rather than biblical times; the normal host of trichina is the rat. The pig was sacrosanct, hence "unclean." Some forbidden fish resembled serpents and were also taboo.

The injunction against cooking a kid in its mother's milk (Exod. 23:19, 34:26, Deut. 14:21) is a literal one, probably because of its connection with idolatrous Canaanite feasts which Moses did not want his people to emulate. Arabs still prepare a special delicacy—*lebban ummho* (literally "the milk of his mother") by cooking a newly born kid in *lebban* or sour milk.[1]

This injunction served as a basis for early rabbinical decrees against mixing milk and meat products, but a minority faction of Jews did not accept such extensions of biblical prohibitions and eventually separated from the main body of Jews and have survived as the Karaites (from *kara*— "to read"—i.e. only what was to be read in the Pentateuch was binding). Karaites eat meat and milk together. Since the establishment of the State of Israel they are being reabsorbed into Judaism.

Whatever the sanitary values of the Mosaic laws, many serious epidemics afflicted the Hebrews if one may judge from the different terms used (*davar, magefah, nega, maka, ketev*) to describe various plagues.

### Plague

There appears to be some evidence that the biblical area also suffered visitations from bubonic plague. Chapters 5 and 6 of Samuel record an outbreak of "emerods" among the Philistines of Ashdod at a time of rat infestation (the Hebrew term in 1 Sam. 6:5 rendered "mice" refers to any rodent). The emerods in this instance were probably buboes of plague. The Septuagint renders 1 Sam. 5:6 rather differently to the Authorized Version, and notes that "The Lord . . . smote them with emerods, and in the midst of the land thereof mice were brought forth, and there was a great and deadly destruction in the city."

As a consequence, the Philistines returned the captured Ark of the Lord to the Hebrews of Bethshemesh, who promptly also suffered an epidemic, and though the deaths were stated to number 50,070 (1 Sam. 6:19), the first century historian, Josephus, puts the figure at the more sensible 70 dead. Perhaps rats accompanied the Philistine retinue to Bethshemesh, or possibly infected fleas were carried on the cows bringing the sacred Ark back to Israel.

It is also probable that bubonic plague decimated Sennacherib's Assyrian who came down like a wolf on the fold with cohorts all gleaming in purple and gold to lay siege to Jerusalem. The historian Herodotus (2:141) observed that the Assyrian camp suffered a plague of "mice" at that time.

### Leprosy

Leprosy must have worried the Israelites a good deal, though the accuracy of their diagnoses will always remain problematical. If one can judge from the facial appearance on a Canaanite jar[2] leonine leprous facies must have occurred. Indeed, the representations of Babylonian evil demons look remarkably leprous. Perhaps the frequent cases at that time of nodular facial leprosy served as a repulsive model for their caricature as demons.

There are many biblical references to lepers, even among captains and kings (2 Kings 5ff, 2 Chron. 26:19ff, Matt. 8:2–3, 10:8, 11:5, Mark 1:40–42, Luke 5:12–13, 7:22, 17:12). They were recognized to be unclean, and had to live outside the camp and the city (Num. 5:2, 2 Kings 7:3) while

*71*

they were still infectious: "All the days wherein the plague shall be in him shall he be defiled; he is unclean: he shall dwell alone; without the camp shall his habitation be" (Lev. 13:46). Even any doubtful marks on a garment from a leprous house rendered it liable to burning (Lev. 13:47–59).

The Hebrews were not alone in regarding leprosy as contagious; indeed the Chaldees, whence came Abraham, also considered leprosy to be infectious and banished the afflicted from the community.

Instructions on the diagnosis of suspicious lesions were given to the priests: "If a man . . . or a woman have in the skin of their flesh bright spots . . ." (Lev. 13:38). Thereafter follow clinical details on differential diagnosis which are not unreasonable.

When healing occurred, a rite of cleansing and purification was mandatory. During the time of Herod the purification ritual took place in a special Court of the Lepers.

Since the cure of leprosy permitted admission to the sanctuary, the arbiter of cure was the priest. It is understandable that Christ should tell ten cured lepers "Go show yourselves unto the priests" (Luke 17:14).

Lazarus (Luke 16:20) the beggar, was "full of sores," traditionally leprous. The first leper houses were established by Christian ascetics in the 8th century. They pictured the condition as in Luke 16:20 so that the leper hospitals were known as Lazar Houses or Lazarettos.

### Enteritis

The "plague" threatening children (2 Chron. 21:14) is commonly misinterpreted to be diarrhea. In fact it referred to military defeat (Verse 17). The diarrhea was suffered by the king alone (Verse 18). Diarrhea was probably not too uncommon; certainly Babylonian physicians are known to have prescribed for it. The temple priests handling carcasses were especially prone to enteritis.[3] Lev. 11:35 requires that food-containing vessels defiled by reptiles such as lizards should be destroyed, and any food therein was also to be taboo. In this regard it is of interest that in East Africa, house lizards are endemic carriers of *Salmonella* pathogenic to man.

The Children of Israel had a hard time, medically speaking, in the wilderness. No sooner did the survivors of an obscure plague (Num. 11:1–3) recover sufficiently to complain about the monotony of their diet of manna, and crave for flesh, fish, cucumbers, melons, leeks, onions and garlic (Num. 11:4,5), than an exasperated God gave them their protein in the form of huge stacks of migratory birds, quail, upon which the people feasted and, as a consequence, suffered another disastrous plague, the nature of which is again obscure but was probably an enteritis of sorts. Some species of fowl also harbor *Salmonella* pathogenic to man, while it is more than likely that the putrefying quail flesh acted as an incubator of infectious enteral organisms.

It has also been suggested that in susceptible people, quail flesh can produce a fatal myoglobinuria. It seems unlikely that this was the cause of the epidemic; it did not occur during an earlier feasting on quail (Exod. 16:13).

Dysentery is recorded in Acts 28:8.

## Typhoid

After years of privation in the wilderness, the Israelites rebelled against their lot, so "the Lord sent fiery serpents among the people, and they bit the people; and much people of Israel died. Therefore the people came to Moses, and said, We have sinned, for we have spoken against the Lord, and against thee; pray unto the Lord, that he take away the serpents from us. And Moses prayed for the people. And the

Lord said unto Moses, Make thee a fiery serpent, and set it upon a pole: and it shall come to pass that every one that is bitten, when he looketh upon it, shall live" (Num. 21:6–8).

The rabbis have had a hard time of it explaining away this bit of God-ordained idolatry. But where the clerics have failed, the doctors—reversing the usual process—have stepped in. Some physicians have suggested that the epidemic was a massive infestation with guinea worms, endemic in the area, and that by entwining a serpent upon a staff, Moses was demonstrating how to extract the long worms from the extremities.

The guinea worm theory has a major drawback: it fails to explain the serious character of the epidemic, clearly of a grievous nature and associated with a heavy mortality. A better explanation involves a short digression on worms.

Up until the 19th century worms were generally held to be responsible for numerous illnesses, especially those associated with fever, for worms were then passed when they were not even suspected to be present.

Among the ancients, worms had a close link with illness, for three reasons:

1. The worm appears to be a diminutive relation of the serpent with its venom.

2. Worms and maggots are present in dead bodies, the inference being drawn that they entered during life and were responsible for demise.

3. Worms were especially prevalent in the sick, and if there was no other obvious cause for illness, could conveniently be blamed.

Both Herod Agrippa (Acts 12:23) and Antiochus Epiphanes (2 Macc. 9:9) died as a consequence of affliction by worms.

The "fiery serpents" in the wilderness were worms. It is relevant to note that the Hebrew adjective is not derived

74

from *esh* (fire) but from *soref* (burn), and it was not the worms that were burning, but the patients who were burning with fever. The worms were especially evident not only because they migrate during fever, but also because diarrhea was part of the illness. Moreover, the worms did not literally bite; the Hebrew term, *nashokh* can also mean "adhere to," "stick to" (Talmud: Mishnah Khallah 2:4, Mishnah Tohoroth 1:7), and in this context it is clear that the fever-producing worms remained long in the Hebrew camp, causing a protracted epidemic. A grave illness of epidemic proportions, lingering among the population, and featuring noteworthy fever, diarrhea, and many deaths, is likely to be typhoid. Cholera is less likely, since fever is usually slight or absent.

One of the arts of the physician is to contrive to be called in, or to administer a remedy, just before the recovery phase sets in. Moses evidently knew of the credit accruing to one who enters the clinical picture at this critical stage. He erected the serpent upon the staff when the epidemic had already run its course.

In the desert the complaining Hebrews were struck down by another feverish illness the nature of which is not clear. A fire of the Lord burned among the people and consumed them (Num. 11:1–3). The words used (*esh*—fire; *ba'ar*—burn) do not recall arguments in favor of typhoid fever.

### Various Feverish Illnesses

Fever (Matt. 8:14, Mark 1:30, Luke 4:38, John 4:52) is called in biblical Hebrew *kadahat* (Lev. 26:16, Deut, 28:22), also translated as "burning ague," and could refer to any markedly pyrexial disease like typhoid or malaria. The Hebrew *daleket* (Deut. 28:22), rendered as "inflammation," has a connotation in the Greek translation of "intermittent fever" and might fit malaria or relapsing fever better. *Harhur,* used only once in the Bible (Deut. 28:22), probably indicates a desiccating heat (dehydration?).

The 5th plague in Egypt, called "murrain" (Exod. 9:3), has been thought by various commentators to refer to anthrax or to trypanosomiasis. This last theory can gain support from the modern view that the third plague (*kinim,* Hebrew) was not lice (Exod. 8:16, Ps. 105:31) but mosquitoes. It is tempting to suggest that the first plague, water to blood, was a form of sympathetic magic stemming from the frequency of bilharzia in Egypt. Round about 1910 Sir Marc Ruffer discovered calcified bilharzia eggs in the kidneys of a mummy from the 20th dynasty. The 6th plague (Exod. 9), translated as "boils" (Hebrew: *shechin*), was probably an epidemic affliction like yaws. The "boils" were more likely open suppurative lesions.

Smallpox has been identified in an Egyptian mummy and there have been theories that Job suffered from it.

Dogs are mentioned in the Bible but there is no record of rabies, a disease known to have occurred in antiquity.

Trachoma was probably endemic in the ancient Near East. Some consider that Paul's thorn in the flesh (2 Cor. 12:7–10) could have referred to the trachoma which first sorely afflicted him when he lost his sight on the way to Damascus. The apocryphal Tobit (2:10–12, 11:13–15), about the 3rd century B.C.E., may have had trachoma and this might also have been the cause of Leah's tender eyes (Gen. 29:17). (Be that as it may, whatever the nature of her ocular disability, one can venture the suggestion that her peers doubtless blamed her eye disease on the fact that her room was not kept sufficiently darkened during her bout of childhood measles. Myths about measles are very old.)

### *Poliomyelitis*

The author of Prov. 26:7 may have been thinking of the ravages of polio when he wrote "The legs of the lame are not equal . . ." However, this translation of the Hebrew makes no sense when taken in conjunction with the rest of the sentence: "so is a parable in the mouth of fools." Admittedly the Hebrew *dalyu* is a difficult term, but it can probably best be rendered "weak," "limp" or "useless," or alternatively "misshapen" or "contorted and contracted," so that this passage would be better rendered "As contorted as are the thighs of a cripple, so is a parable in the mouth of fools."

Poliomyelitis has been identified in Egypt at the time of Moses.

Very likely the lad Mephibosheth (2 Sam. 4:4) had polio. This is reasonably clear from a perusal of the Hebrew text. The English translation is misleading so that some writers have wondered whether he did not suffer a fractured spine as a consequence of a fall. In the Authorized Version the term "lame" is used to translate two distinct Hebrew words. The passage would be better rendered "And Jonathan . . . had a son that was lame of his feet (*nekheh raglaim*) . . . and . . . he fell, and became crippled (*vayipaseakh*)."

Presumably poliomyelitis had rendered him lame prior to the fall which cracked one or more decalcified bones in the affected leg, and crippled him.

Crippling for one or other reason must have been common and crutches were used. The celebrated passage in 1 Kings 18:21 "How long will ye halt between two opinions?" is more literally rendered as "How long will ye halt between two crutches?" The Hebrew *se'if* means a branch or a crutch.

A number of passages in the New Testament (e.g., the

77

man with the withered hand, Mark 3:1–5) can be interpreted in terms of polio, but they are all mere guesses; there is insufficient clinical detail.

## Tuberculosis

It has been suggested that Abraham emigrated from his native Ur in order to escape from widespread tuberculosis there. The Hebrew *shakhephet* (Lev. 26:16, Deut. 28:22), rendered "consumption," is derived from a root meaning "to become thin." *Kalah* (Zech. 14:12) has a similar connotation. Tuberculosis was known in Egypt and it has been suggested that the youthful Tutankhamen may have been a victim of adolescent phthisis. If the "croockbackt" of Lev. 21:20 refers to a collapsed tuberculous spine (rickets must have been rare in sunny Palestine) then tuberculosis may have been common enough for Moses to legislate that hunchbacks were not to defile the sanctuary.

There is no basis to theories[4] that the Hebrews had no tuberculosis because there is no biblical term for cough. This view is not only medically unsound but is also philologically untrue. The *zarar* of 2 Kings 4:35, translated as "sneeze," can mean any spasmodic respiratory sound, and in fact the episode of the recovery of the Shunemite child in this passage makes better sense if cough is substituted for sneeze.

There is a sound philological basis for such a medical speculation. The term *zarar* is a *hapax legomenon;* it occurs only once in the Bible and is never repeated, though Isa. 1:6 makes use of the root *zr (zoru)* to indicate a wound whose edges have been closed up or squeezed together.

The Septuagint, possibly because of difficulty in translation, leaves out *zarar* altogether and renders the passage as follows "And he returned and walked up and down in the house; and he went up, and bowed himself upon the child seven times . . . and the child opened his eyes."

If the root *zr* originally connoted a squeeze then the possibility of extension of meaning to include cough is by no means remote. Such a development is comprehensible in the context of a cough as a paroxysmal mechanism for squeezing air out of the chest. Sneezing would also fall into this category. The Aramaic *zerira* means sneeze, but the same root in Arabic means to wink with the eyes, also a paroxysmal closure.[5]

A later Hebrew word, *atash,* is used a few hundred years after *zarar* was first employed, and unquestionably *atash* (Job 41:18) means sneeze. The Coptic for sneeze is *antas*.[5]

### Skin and Venereal Disease

Skin lesions such as sepsis, boils and abscesses (Gen. 34:25, Exod. 9:9, Isa. 38:21, 2 Kings 20:7, Rev. 16:2) and stinking wounds (Job 7:5, Isa. 1:6, Luke 16:20,21) as well as osteomyelitis (Prov. 12:4, 14:30, Hab. 3:16) are recorded, while all sorts of superficial skin lesions, from parasitic infections to dermatitis herpetiformis have been thought to have afflicted the long-suffering Job.

"Job never existed; the book is a parable" (Talmud, Baba Bathra 15a). When we speak Job's illness we really speak of the clinical picture in the mind of the author of the book. It seems that he was thinking of a picture rather like that of yaws and some good pieces of evidence support this diagnosis. His alleged "boils" (the Hebrew is a non-specific *shechin*) are called, in the Septuagint, "foul ulcers" (2:7). He scraped the itchy lesions with a piece of broken pottery (2:8), a method of relief still practised by Beduin sufferers in the Middle East. Egyptians still call the yaws-syphilis complex *Manes Ayoub,* the malady of Job. It is clear however that Job was faithful to his one wife (31:1,9) so that syphilis is much less likely than yaws.

The two diseases are surprisingly alike, both having evanescent primary lesions (non-venereal in the case of yaws), a secondary stage lasting some weeks or months, and tertiary bony or central nervous system consequences. In yaws the most prominent manifestations occur during the secondary stage, which features large, foul, crusted, itchy ulcers. Constitutional symptoms may also occur, especially pain, tenderness and swelling of the bones, fever and disturbed sleep.

Job is accurate in his descriptions: "my skin is broken, and become loathsome" (*vayima'ess,* literally "has sloughed off" 7:5). He had multiple lesions (9:17). He complains bitterly about his painful bones (2:5, 19:20, 33:19) which are "burned with heat" (30:30) especially at night: "My bones are pierced in me in the night season: and my sinews take no rest" (30:17). He cannot sleep: "wearisome nights are appointed to me. When I lie down, I say, When shall I arise, and the night be gone? and I am full of tossings to and fro unto the dawnings of the day" (7:3,4). He cannot eat (33:20) and is wasting away (33:21).

Job could have been successfully treated with extracts of hyssop. It has already been noted that the mold *Penicillium notatum* grows on this shrub.

Syphilitic changes have not been observed in any bones from Egyptian mummies, and the presence of syphilis in ancient Israel is problematical. One is sorely tempted to diagnose King David as a syphilitic. If Psalm 38 is his—it is headed "A Psalm of David"—then he gives a reasonable description of his shooting pains, his gummatous wounds and his iritis, all as a consequence of his indiscretion with Bathsheba: "There is no soundness in my flesh . . . neither is there any rest in my bones because of my sin . . . My

wounds stink and are corrupt because of my foolishness . . .
my loins are filled with a burning (Jewish Publication
Society of America translation) . . . My heart panteth . . .
as for the light of mine eyes, it is also gone from me . . ."

It is possible to draw venereal conclusions from vastly
insufficient evidence. In Jer. 31:29 (see also Ezek. 18:2) it is
written "The fathers have eaten a sour grape, and the children's teeth are set on edge." It is really too much to suggest,
as does Brim[6] that the fathers have contracted syphilis and
the children have Hutchinson teeth!

Some writers have seen syphilitic possibilities in a number of biblical passages (Num. 5:22–27, 31:17–18, Josh.
22:17, Prov. 7:23,26, Sira 19:3) and especially in Num. 12:12
which describes a macerated fetus.

The matter of emerods (see under "Plague") also lends
itself to alternative explanation. The Hebrew term used in
various passages is *opholim* (singular, *ophal*) though in 1
Sam. 6:11 *tekhorim* is substituted (is *opholim* too obscene?).
Babylonian and Arabic derivations of *ophal* mean boil, while
Syriac, Arabic and Aramaic roots related to *tekhorim* refer
either to the rectum or to defecation.[b] Probably emerods
refer to any swelling in the genital area. One writer regards
the emerods of Deut. 28:27,28 as syphilitic condylomata:
"The Lord shall smite thee with the boil of Egypt, and . . .
emerods . . . The Lord shall smite thee with madness, and
blindness and astonishment of heart." and continues to suggest that if the first part of the sentence refers to the initial
manifestations of lues, then the rest is surely prophetic of the
later manifestations.[7]

If David had syphilis, why not gonorrhea as well? His
first wife, Michal, remained sterile all her life (2 Sam. 6:23).
One must consider the distressing possibility that the handsome dashing young David at the court of King Saul had
given her gonococcal salpingitis, as a consequence of which

she was not even fertile by her second husband (1 Sam. 25:44).

Gonorrhea is noted in the bible as "an issue" and stringent purification in both man and woman is described in detail in the whole of Lev. 15. It is revealing that there are several references (Lev. 22:4, Num. 5:2, 2 Sam. 3:29) to an "issue" coupled with an eruption which is called by the non-specific term leprosy, but which is better understood as syphilitic, for syphilis and gonorrhea commonly coexist.

If one can indict David on the basis of his spouse's sterility, one must also consider the possibility that Abraham was similarly afflicted. Both his wife Sarah and his concubine Hagar fell pregnant only once. Moreover, when Sarah had an affair with Abimelech (the biblical writer is suspiciously quick to deny intimacy: Gen. 20:3,4) he proceeded to hand around gonococcal salpingitis to his harem: "For the Lord had fast closed up (literally?) all the wombs of the house of Abimelech . . ." (20:18).

When one considers that at least one recent Middle Eastern potentate is known to have had venereal disease, could Solomon have escaped gonorrhea?

## REFERENCES

1. Masterman, E. W. G. (1920): *Hygiene and Disease in Palestine in Modern and in Biblical Times.* Palestine Expl. Fund, London

2. Yoeli, M. (1968): *Bulletin of the New York Academy of Medicine,* 44: 1057

3. Corswant, W. (1960): *A Dictionary of Life in Bible Times.* Transl. by A. Heathcote. Hodder & Stoughton, London

4. Smith, E. R. (1960): *British Journal of Diseases of the Chest,* 54: 226

5. van Selms, A. Professor of Semitic Languages, University of Pretoria, (1959): Personal communication

6. Brim, C. J. (1936): *Medicine in the Bible.*  Froben Press, New York

7. Willcox, R. R. (1949): *British Journal of Venereal Diseases,* 25: 28

# METABOLISM AND MISCELLANEA

With just a little imagination one can recognize some biblical disturbances of endocrine function. In addition to the celebrated Goliath, one Og, King of Bashan, was also a giant (Deut. 3:11) and some giants peopled the earth in the early days of Genesis (6:4). If the 6-fingered giant of Gath (2 Sam. 21:20) also had difficulty with vision (after all a more nimble foe slew him: v. 21) a diagnosis of Laurence-Moon-Biedl syndrome may legitimately be entertained. There were other giants in his company (2 Sam. 21:16–22).

If the text is not corrupted, King Ahaz must have been a pituitary giant, and a father at the age of 11 years. When he died at the age of 36 years (2 Kings 16:2,20) his son was already 25 years old (2 Kings 18:2).

Dwarfs (Lev. 21:20) and progressive dwarfism (2 Esd. 5:54,55) are noted.

Any physical deformity whatever (Lev. 21:17–23, Deut. 23:1) rendered one ritually unacceptable for temple duties.

Cryptorchidism is implied in Matt. 19:12. Esau had hirsuties and (so some biblical commentators infer) large genitals (Gen. 25:27) which Brim[1] thinks is sufficient to label him as a case of adrenogenital syndrome. It is even conceivable that he had hypoglycemia and dehydration (Gen. 25:29, 30,32).

With a little imagination it is possible to diagnose an episode of hunger hypoglycemia relieved by honey: "But Jonathan heard not when his father charged the people with the oath: wherefore he put forth the end of the rod that was in his hand, and dipped it in an honey-comb, and put his hand to his mouth; and his eyes were enlightened" (1 Sam. 14:27).

Taub [2] gives reasons for diagnosing the men of Anak (Num. 13:33, the word means "neck") as goitrous.

There is even a suggestion of factors predisposing to mongolism: "Those born in the strength of youth are different to those born during the time of old age, when the womb is failing." (2 Esd. 5:51–53). Feeblemindedness is mentioned in Ps. 116:6, Jer. 4:22 and 1 Thess. 5:14.

Visions of diabetes mellitus are conjured up by Lev. 26:26 "and they shall deliver you your bread . . . by weight: and ye shall eat, and not be satisfied."

A number of endocrine or glandular defects can be considered in greater detail:

## *Joseph*

As a youth Joseph must have been somewhat effeminate, a conclusion reached by the 11th century French rabbi, Rashi, perhaps the greatest of biblical commentators. Rashi wrote that Joseph combed and smoothed his hair and liked to enhance his looks.

His physical appearance is described as pretty (Gen. 39:6) and, significantly, the descriptive adjectives in the Hebrew are precisely those used to denote the beauty of his mother (29:17), grandmother (24:16) and great-grandmother (12:11). He liked pretty clothes (37:3) and his long-sleeved coat (NOT a coat of many colors) was of the type worn by a girl (2 Sam. 13:18). However, this last does not necessarily indicate a feminine outlook in the matter of clothes. Such a garment was the hallmark of royalty and aristocracy.

Nevertheless, he gossiped (Gen. 37:2) and Rashi comments that he complained to his father about the lewdness of his brothers.

At the age of 17 years, he experienced sexual (?) dreams with phallic symbolism, his sheaf only standing erect (37:5–11). He was pampered by his doting father (37:3) and, though 17 years old was still called a *naar,* a boy, a lad, though to be sure this does not necessarily indicate immaturity: in 2 Sam. 2:14 this same term *naar* clearly refers to a warrior.

Nevertheless, the overall impression is that of a good-looking effeminate "tattle-tale" loved and spoilt by his parents.

### Saul

Was Saul mad? Did the King have periods when he was psychotic? So it is generally thought: "King Saul would be diagnosed now as a typical example of manic-depressive insanity. The periods of intense gloom with occasional outbreaks of homicidal violence for no particular reason, as when he hurled his javelin at David and it fixed itself in the wall behind, the delusions that people in general and David most of all were plotting against him, and the suicide at the end, are unmistakable." [3] Dr. Smith concurs with this diagnosis. [4] Also in favor of insanity is the statement of 1 Sam. 16:14, 18:10, 19:9 that an "evil spirit" troubled Saul, and Josephus in the first century wrote that Saul was demon-possessed. Demons and spirits were commonly associated with mental and epileptic manifestations. King David feigned insanity before Achish, King of Gath (1 Sam. 21:13–15). Perhaps this ruse sprang to mind because he had been made constantly aware of madness during his association with Saul.

David's state however, is described by the Hebrew word *meshugah,* a term not used with respect to Saul.

Saul was an unstable and unpredictable character. A zealously devout battler on behalf of his God, he fought against wizardry, occultism and sorcery, yet was not above indulging in necromancy (1 Sam. 28:7ff) and in losing himself in religious trances among itinerant seers (10:10, 19:24). More than once he lent his fervent intensity to the roving bands of ecstatic prophets so that his behavior became a byword in Israel: "Is Saul also among the prophets?" (10:11,12, 19:24) was an idiom used to describe the unexpected behavior of men of high station found acting disreputably in questionable company.

No doubt Saul was an impetuous man, but were his moods fits of melancholia, or something else?

Saul is first encountered as (possibly) the young man who fought at Aphek (4:2). When crowned King over Israel, he was a notably tall and strong man, probably about 40 years of age, for his eldest son Jonathan was in his late teens, having recently married. At the age of 45 years Saul had consolidated his kingdom, and at this time he required David, then perhaps 18 years, to play before him.

Some 3 years later, David again appeared on the scene to take credit for the Goliath affair and rejoin the court of Saul. As David's star rose, so did Saul's suspicion—and his javelin. For perhaps 4 years Saul harried David, and finally met his end on the mountains of Gilboa in his early fifties.

Saul's alleged melancholia wasn't manifest until his middle forties. Before that his unusual stature was a noteworthy feature (9:2). It is suggested that Saul had acromegalic gigantism beginning in his late teens. His slow-growing pituitary tumor, however, did not reach significant proportions until the age of perhaps 45 years when episodes of headache worried him and were soothed by David's harp

(16:23), or else the tunes provided a sufficient diversion from his misery. Three years later, attacks were so severe that one can well understand onlookers concluding that an evil spirit had entered into him. Tormented by raging headaches, which David's harp increasingly failed to relieve or divert, and increasingly suspicious of David's popularity, the exasperated King twice hurled his javelin at David and, able warrior though he was, twice missed (18:11, 19:10) at close range; this is not surprising for Saul could no longer see well, a large pituitary tumor impairing peripheral vision.

Insanity explains one feature of Saul's behavior; acromegaly explains three: gigantism, headaches and poor vision.

## In a Manner of Speaking

Mention of Saul provides this opportunity to consider in a little more detail the phenomenon of jabbering ecstatic speech, and of speech disorders in general.

Quite apart from the ordinary uses of voice in the Bible, unusual manifestations of speech are recorded under three groups of circumstances:
1. Non-human speech.
2. Glossolalia.
3. Other Speech Defects.

### Non-Human Speech

God, Satan, angels and other extra-human celestial creatures speak from time to time in the pages of the scriptures. Perhaps the most powerful of God's words to any mortal is the awesome voice out of the whirlwind with its crushing question to Job: "Who is this that darkeneth counsel by words without knowledge?" (Job 38:1,2).

God spoke gently to the child Eli (1 Sam. 3:10) and a voice from heaven confirmed Jesus as God's beloved son (Mark 1:11).

Of the speaking animals, the serpent that beguiled Eve (Gen. 3:1 ff) is justly the most notorious. Balaam's ass (Num. 22:28, 2 Pet. 2:16) complained loudly and bitterly to his master. Even the trees got together (Judg. 9:8–15) to elect one of their number to govern them.

## Glossolalia

There is a large body of apologetic theological writing on glossolalia, or "speaking with tongues," a phenomenon recorded a number of times in the New Testament and most clearly in Acts 2:1–11:

"And when the day of Pentecost was fully come, they were all with one accord in one place. And suddenly there came a sound from heaven as of a rushing mighty wind, and it filled all the house where they were sitting. And there appeared unto them cloven tongues like as of fire, and it sat upon each of them. And they were all filled with the Holy Ghost, and began to speak with other tongues, as the Spirit gave them utterance. And there were dwelling at Jerusalem Jews, devout men, out of every nation under heaven. Now when this was noised abroad, the multitude came together, and were confounded, because that every man heard them speak in his own language . . . we do hear them speak in our tongues the wonderful works of God."

Though it may be difficult for modern minds to accept the truth and historicity of such a record (and hence the apologetic literature) it seems that the intention was in fact to indicate that the disciples spoke spontaneously and intelligibly in various languages previously unknown to them. More likely they were moved by religious fervor to incomprehensible babbling which the author (Luke, in the case of Acts) considered was real, and a gift of the Holy Spirit. Paul had his misgivings about glossolalia and discouraged it (1 Cor. 14:19), but a number of sects practised it all throughout Christian history and at present Apostolic and Pentecostal adherents are still moved by religious rapture to outbursts of inarticulate sounds.

The phenomenon was not new to the Jewish Christians who made up the early Jerusalem Church. It was also known to the earlier Hebrews. Bands of seers and "prophets" commonly roamed the countryside, losing themselves every so often in ecstatic dance and voice, perhaps in the manner of Moslem dervishes. More than once King Saul joined the revels of these seers.

The best-known glossolalia is in the babble of Babel. The story of the Tower of Babel (Gen. 11:1–9) purports to explain the multiplicity of languages on earth. As a consequence of the intended assault on heaven by the people of Shinar (Babylonia), God confused their tongues so that they could not understand each other, and hence could no longer cooperate in their nefarious venture. Those who babbled the same tongues separated themselves to form groups and nations. The biblical writer includes a tradition of popular etymology in order to explain the name Babel, playing on the superficial similarity between this word and the Hebrew term for "confusion." In fact, the name is made up of *Bab-el,* "gate of god."

## Other Speech Defects

Isaiah refers a few times (28:11, 32:4, 33:19) to stuttering and Moses complained that he was "slow of speech, and of a slow tongue" (Exod. 4:10), a condition which has been widely interpreted to betoken stuttering. A Talmudic legend relates that the infant Moses was tested by a suspicious Pharaoh who offered him a choice of a crown (in which case his life was forfeit) or a hot coal. Moses placed the coal on his tongue and burnt it, and as a result had a lifelong impediment of speech.

Adam was a stutterer, the origin of his speech defect having been considered in the first chapter.

Mark (7:32) refers to "one that was deaf, and had an impediment in his speech" miraculously cured by Christ so that "his ears were opened, and the string of his tongue was loosed, and he spake plain" (7:35). Others who were dumb were also cured (Matt. 9:33, 12:22). Zacharias temporarily lost his voice (John 1:22, 64).

An impediment of speech was common in the tribe of Ephraim. They could not easily pronounce "sh," saying "s" instead. When Ephraimite fugitives were fleeing from Jephtha and the soldiers of Gilead, before being permitted to cross a ford on the Jordan the suspected Ephraimites were asked to pronounce *"shibboleth"* (meaning: a stream in flood). Those saying *"sibboleth"* were slaughtered (Judg. 12:1–6).


## Paul

Mention of Paul's attitude to glossolalia brings up the question of the sickness that plagued him all his adult life.

The nature of his disability is not at all clear. Many commentators have thought him to be an epileptic: this on the basis of his supposedly pre-convulsive visions. Yet there is no mention of demons afflicting him, nor of anything which may be construed to be of epileptic nature.

When Paul speaks of "a thorn in the flesh, the messenger of Satan to buffet me" (2 Cor. 12:7) he appears to imply some obvious disability, visible to the eye and perhaps even present in his flesh. In fact this view seems quite clear from Gal. 4:14. "You resisted any temptation to show scorn or disgust at the state of my poor body" (New English Bible). He describes his physiognomy as unimpressive or "weak" (2 Cor. 10:10).

We may take cognizance of a few other physical details:

Paul had some trouble with his eyes. As a result of his Damascus-bound experience he was blind for three days, and subsequently "there fell from his eyes as it had been scales" (Acts 9:9,18). His desire for the eyes of others (Gal. 4:15) is a proverbial expression, yet possibly grounded in fact. Paul had difficulty (visual?) in recognizing the high priest (Acts 23:5).

Nobody reading Paul's writings can doubt his astuteness. At times his use of words is masterful. Yet he calls his speech "contemptible" (2 Cor. 10:10) and "rude" (11:6). Certainly not humble or reticent, his descriptions of his own manner of speaking may refer to hesitancy or other impediments of speech.

Paul was unmarried (1 Cor. 7:7–8) yet he knew of passion (7:9). It is difficult to believe that a young Jew of that time could have resisted the intense parental and religious pressures to marry. Being single, he either would not—an unlikely possibility—or else could not marry. If, as is probably likely, he adhered from an early age to one or other pagan mystery cult advocating celibacy (repudiation of sex was a condition of admission to some cults), then his reasons for not marrying (1 Cor. 7:27–40) make sense; on the other hand, his arguments may be rationalizations stemming from the distressing finding that he had tried and found that he could not. Impotence is at least a possibility.

Paul also had psychiatric aberrations. He had intense spiritual experiences (2 Cor. 12:1–7) and took pride in them (Rom. 15:19, 2 Cor. 12:12). Though he decried "speaking with tongues" he nevertheless also experienced ecstatic glossolalia (1 Cor. 14:18). Paul himself wondered about his own sanity (2 Cor. 5:13).

His biographer Luke describes Paul's Damascus hallucination and includes another vision at Corinth (Acts 18:9). Procurator Festus recognized him to be unbalanced (Acts 26:24). The rational Greeks of Athens laughed him to scorn (Acts 17:32).

On these factors alone no diagnosis is possible, but if we make use of an apocryphal description of Paul, a diagnosis becomes possible. In a popular romance of the 2nd century known as The Acts of Paul and Thecla, Paul is described as "A man little of stature, thin-haired upon the head, crooked in the legs, of good state of body, with eyebrows joining, and nose somewhat hooked, full of grace."

Dystrophia myotonica is a form of muscular dystrophy characterized by stiffness and wasting of the muscles of the limbs, neck and face, testicular atrophy, frontal baldness, cataract and occasionally psychiatric disturbances.

It occurs most often in males, starting at the age of 20 to 30 years, progressing very gradually and ending in death in late middle life.

The various disabilities need not be uniformly progressive so that, for example, cataract might appear early, testicular atrophy and impotence might be pronounced shortly after the age of 20 years, whereas incapacitating stiffness and clumsiness might well be delayed to the age of 50 years. The stiffness is often most marked in the muscles of the hands and tongue.

The following features of the disorder were manifest in Paul:

A disability of his fleshy body, of his muscles.

Eye trouble; cataract?

Speech defects consequent on myotonia of his tongue.

*93*

Impotence. The tale of Paul and Thecla, no doubt a pious fabrication, may nevertheless be based on a factual foundation. The girl Thecla made allegedly religious advances to Paul, but he repulsed her.

Psychiatric disturbances.

Baldness.

Bow-legs due to wasting of his muscles.

The prominent nose on a face otherwise full of grace could easily refer to the peculiarly expressionless or mournful facies with smooth forehead consequent on the atrophy of the facial muscles. Interestingly enough, exhibits in Vatican museums feature 4th century representations of Paul on metal and stone. They show a man with frontal baldness, smooth face, unwrinkled brow and decidedly thin neck.

But can one reconcile a muscular dystrophy with a man as restlessly energetic as Paul? He used his hands to good effect: he was a tent-maker (Acts 18:3). He had the stamina to brave all sorts of perils and hardships (2 Cor. 11:23–27) and traveled thousands of miles, perhaps a good deal of it on foot, to spread his gospel throughout the empire of Rome.

It is certainly possible, muscular dystrophy notwithstanding. In determination Paul lacked nothing. Whatever the elements, however hazardous the journey, no matter how weary, Paul pressed on.

For his work was in fact ended before he reached middle age, before his muscular disabilities crippled him. Paul was probably born between 5–10 C.E. and was arrested and imprisoned around 55 C.E. from which time he was effectively removed from personal contact with his converts.

His mission began at about the age of 20–25 years, at which time he was already sickly, and by the age of 50 years he had written his most important epistles, had defined his soteriology, had established churches, had warred with the

Jerusalem faction and posthumously survived their destruction.

In a mere 25 years during which he was spared incapacitating physical disablement, his word sped through the Roman empire and for 2,000 years has thundered round the world.

### *Familial Dysautonomia*

The obscure metabolic or neuromuscular disorder of Paul brings to mind an equally obscure metabolic or neuromuscular disorder first described by Ezekiel and then forgotten about for some 25 centuries, after which, somewhat more than 20 years ago, Dr. C. Riley of New York described this curious and poorly understood illness which he termed "familial dysautonomia."

It is a hereditary disorder, occurring almost exclusively in Jews, and the two cardinal symptoms are an inability to produce tears, and a decreased sensitivity to pain. Among another 10 or 15 features of the condition should be mentioned behavior problems, difficulty with feeding, drooling, coldness of the extremities, corneal anesthesia with ulceration, excessive perspiration, poor speech, odd gait and retardation in growth.

No mean clinician, Ezekiel's findings were as follows: (Addressed to Jews) "Son of man," (hereditary influence) "behold, I take away from thee the desire of thine eyes" (corneal anesthesia with ulceration) "with a stroke:" (pathology in the central nervous system) "yet neither shalt thou mourn" (incongruous behavioral response) "nor weep," (insensitivity to pain) "neither shall thy tears run down" (failure of lacrymation) (24:16).

Some seven features of the disease are thus described in

*95*

but one sentence, probably sufficient to give the prophet priority. Perhaps Riley's syndrome is better renamed Ezekiel's Curse.

## Lot's Wife

Metabolic disorders refer more particularly to malfunctioning of the fluids and chemicals within the body.

The most spectacular such malfunction befell the spouse of Lot, the nephew of Abraham. Lot is famous not so much for the escapades of his daughters (Gen. 19:30–38) but for the fate of his wife. She looked back and became a pillar of salt (Gen. 19:26).

At the southern end of the Dead Sea massive columns of solid salt rise above the bleak mounds which Beduin still call *Jebel Usdum* (the mountain of Sodom). One gaunt pillar looks vaguely human, so that it is easy to picture an itinerant sage inventing the tale of Lot's wife to enthrall his wide-eyed grandchildren.

The ethical dilemma of her fate is usually hurriedly skirted. Here was a woman, unlike the other inhabitants of Sodom and Gomorrah, who had dealt kindly and hospitably with the emissaries of God, and lo! her reward was salty petrification. What manner of justice is this? "Shall not the Judge of all the Earth do right?" (Gen. 18:25)

Actually she was paid a handsome compliment. Salt was considered especially important to the deity (Lev. 2:13). A "covenant of salt" united God and man (Num. 18:19, 2 Chron. 13:5). This covenant stresses the solemn, solid, irrevocable character of the relationship established, in this case between God and the Moabite and Ammonite offspring of the daughters born to Lot's wife.

Salt also makes soil unproductive and Semites often

sowed it over the sites of cities they had destroyed (Judg. 9:45).

The wifely pillar of salt thus typified God's affection and it was established where none could overgrow it. In her eerie realm, haughty and alone, the stark presence of Lot's wife reveals the thoughtfulness and gratitude of the deity who preserved her virtue in salt forever.

## The Effects of Heat

There have been suggestions that Ishmael suffered a feverish illness during his journey in the wilderness (Gen. 21). It is inconceivable that his father Abraham could have sent him and his mother away while he was ill; so that Ishmael must have had a sudden feverish illness, and, as a consequence of this, his fluid requirements in a hot environment markedly increased, and the water supply was soon exhausted. Hagar placed him under a shrub and God then indicated a well of water from which the lad assuaged his thirst and made a rapid recovery.

The fever as well as the heat caused excessive perspiration with loss of sweat containing proportionately little electrolyte, so that Ishmael suffered hypertonic dehydration. Treated in a physiologically correct manner, he made a rapid recovery.

The 3-year-old Shunemite child (2 Kings 4) who suffered from heat stroke while learning to reap in a particularly hot summer valley, also suffered hypertonic dehydration as a consequence of his profuse perspiration.

Manasseh also died at the time of the barley harvest: "he was overcome by the burning heat, and took to his bed and died" (Judith 8:3). Jonah fainted from the heat of the sun (4:8). Isaiah (49:10) refers to the injurious effects of heat and sun and illustrates an example of a smith working with tongs and hammers over an oven of hot coals, drinking insufficient water and feeling faint (44:12).

## *Dehydration*

Not only heat is responsible for dehydration, but other disturbances of water and salt balance as well. When the men of Jericho complained about a water supply, Elisha poured salt therein, uttering, on behalf of his God "I have healed these waters" (2 Kings 2:21).

Dehydration and marasmus ("I can count all my bones") are mentioned in Ps. 22:14,15,17. Dehydration specifically in infants is mentioned in Lam. 4:4: "The tongue of the sucking child cleaveth to the roof of his mouth for thirst." It is tempting to link this passage with the description of gastroenteritis in Lam. 2:11: "My bowels are troubled, my liver is poured upon the earth." However, this association is spurious for it is likely that Lam. 2 and 4 are by different hands even though all of Lamentations is traditionally attributed to Jeremiah.

Sisera came to grief by virtue of his dehydration. He fled in defeat before the victorious arms of the prophetess Deborah. Tired and fearful, dusty and sweating, thirsty and hungry after his headlong flight, he made his way to the tent of Jael and asked for "a little water . . . for I am thirsty" (Judg. 4:19). The wily Jael, contemplating his murder, evidently considered that milk was a better medium to lull her prey to sound sleep and so she gave a fluid with electrolyte and nutrient as well. This episode draws attention to the management of dehydration, electrolyte depletion and hunger. Was Sisera right, physiologically speaking, in asking for water, and was Jael correct in offering milk?

In biochemical terms Jael was a good hostess but a poor

doctor. Her guest and her prey had lost proportionately more water via skin and lungs (we have no reason to believe that Sisera had fibrocystic disease!). Having hypertonic dehydration he voiced his body's needs correctly. Jael gave milk, which also has electrolytes and considerable protein, both inducing an unnecessary renal osmolar load.

Worse still, Jael doubtless gave the milk of a goat or sheep, for there must have been few cows in the hilly country of central Canaan. Sheep and goat's milk contain even more electrolyte, especially phosphate, and also more protein than cow's milk, placing a particularly high excretory strain on the kidneys. Jael's ministrations were unsound, medically speaking, and indeed her patient died, though his demise was expedited by means other than mere electrolyte imbalance!

## REFERENCES

1. Brim, C. J. (1936): *Medicine in the Bible.*   Froben Press, New York
2. Taub, J. (1955) : *The Hebrew Medical Journal.* 2:164
3. Short, A. R. (1953): *The Bible and Modern Medicine.*   Paternoster Press, London
4. Smith, C. R. (1950):   *The Physician Examines the Bible.* Philosophical Library, New York

# MOTHERS AND BABIES

In the Hebrew Bible there is no clear mention or understanding of the concept of an afterlife. A man lived on in his children and his grandchildren. The supreme fulfillment of the Hebrew wife was in motherhood, and the greatest joy and hope of the Hebrew father was for many sons to carry on his seed, his name, and indeed, his very life. The salute "O King, live forever!" (Dan. 2:4) simply meant "O King, may thy seed never die out!" No more terrible curse could befall a man than Jeremiah's "Write ye this man childless!" (22:30). No more dire threat was there than "Seeing thou hast forgotten the law of thy God, I will also forget thy children" (Hos. 4:6, see also Lev. 20:20,21, Job 18:19).

Conversely, there was no blessing as bounteous as "Thy wife shall be as a fruitful vine . . . thy children like olive plants . . ." (Ps. 128:3). Children are likened to trusty arrows: "Happy is the man that hath his quiver full of them" (Ps. 127:5). As payment for righteousness the Psalmist promises a long life in order that "thou shalt see thy children's children" (128:6). Jeremiah notes of a father that ". . . a man child is born . . . making him very glad" (20:15). The ten children born to Job after his harrowing ordeal are sufficient recompense (42:13) and he is supremely happy to see successive generations of his descendants (42:16). The wisdom of Proverbs states that "Children's children are the crown of old men" (17:6). Nathan delivers a glad prophecy to King David: "And when thy days be fulfilled, and thou shalt sleep with thy fathers, I will set up thy seed after thee, which shall proceed out of thy bowels . . ." (2 Sam. 7:12).

Such a picture of literal immortality was quite as satisfying to the early Hebrews as is the modern concept of spiritual survival to the modern believer. Abraham cries: "Lord God, what wilt thou give me, seeing I go childless . . . ?" (Gen. 15:2). So important was progeny, that a man was excused military service for a year after his marriage (Deut. 24:5, see also Deut. 20:7) in order that he could be with his wife until she had time to bear him a child—preferably a son. No more dreadful fate could befall Jeroboam than the loss of his son, because it meant the extinction of his house (1 Kings 14:10). The widow of Tekoah pleads with King David for her sole remaining son, for if the relatives should kill him, they "shall not leave to my husband neither name nor remainder upon the earth" (2 Sam. 14:7).

The father's chief anxiety then, was that he should not die without a son to carry on his name. It was not that daughters were not desired; surely they were, but as the male carried on the paternal line, a son was a necessity for the self-respect of the family.

The mother's central interest too, was the propagation of children—her chief duty, pride and joy. A barren wife had cause for shame, and one with many children could hold her head high.

Tamar, a widow (Gen. 38:18), and both of Lot's daughters (19:36) went to extraordinary lengths in order to become pregnant. So important was the function of childbearing that Judg. 5:30 designates a woman as "a womb." The English translation states "damsel" but the Hebrew word used (*rakham*) means "womb." Hannah, barren, wept and prayed for a child so earnestly that Eli the priest thought her to be drunk (1 Sam. 1:13).

"Give me children," cried Rachel (Gen. 30:1) "or else I die." The harlot of 1 Kings 3 was prepared to give up her infant to another woman rather than see him divided in two. Sarah, in the apocryphal book of Tobit (3:10), contemplates suicide rather than face the possibility of childlessness. Jephtha's daughter bewails not her approaching doom, but the impossibility of fulfilling her womanly function (Judg. 11:37). Elisha asks what request could he grant to the Shunamite woman who had been hospitable to him. Even the King could be approached on her behalf, but her sorrow is that she is barren: "Verily she hath no child, and her husband is old" (2 Kings 4:14). Deutero-Isaiah exults on behalf of the barren who are soon to bear: "Sing, O barren, thou that didst not bear; break forth into singing, and cry aloud, thou that didst not travail with child: for more are" (i.e. more are to be) "the children of the desolate than the children of the married wife" (54:1). "A woman that is in travail hath sorrow" stated Christ "but as soon as she is delivered of the child, she remembereth no more the anguish, for joy that a man is born into the world" (John 16:21).

## God's Role in Pregnancy

Pregnancy is an accident of coitus. Not so simple however, was the Hebrew belief. They considered that children were not merely the result of sexual union, but a direct gift from God.

Of Eve, first mother on earth, it is written ". . . and she bare Cain, and said, I have gotten a man from the Lord" (Gen. 4:1). To Manoah's wife, the Angel of the Lord promised "thou shalt . . . bear a son" (Judg. 13:3). An angel knew that the mother of Jesus would conceive (Luke 2:21).

To Ruth's husband, Boaz, is expressed the hope for "the seed which the Lord shall give thee of this young woman" (Ruth 4:12), and of Ruth it is written that "The Lord gave her conception" (4:13). We read in 1 Sam. 2:21 that "The Lord visited Hannah, so that she conceived."

The Psalmist sings "He maketh the barren woman . . . to be a joyful mother" (113:9). When Rachel cried to Jacob for a child he reproached her "Am I in God's stead, who hath withheld from thee the fruit of the womb?" (Gen. 30:2). Jacob describes his offspring to Esau as "The children which God hath graciously given thy servant" (Gen. 33:5). "Children are an heritage of the Lord: and the fruit of the womb is his reward" (Ps. 127:3). The apocryphal mother who watched the martyrdom of her seven sons cried: "Twas not I who gave you the breath of life or fashioned the elements of each. Twas the Creator of the world who fashioned men and deviseth the generating of all things" (2 Macc. 7:21,22). It is God "who formed man, and put a heart in the midst of his body, and gave him breath and life and understanding" (2 Esd. 16:61). A mother confessed "And after thirty years God . . . gave me a son" (2 Esd. 9:45).

Following naturally from the belief that children were a dispensation from God, we can understand that the treatment of sterility consisted of prayer: "And Isaac entreated the Lord for his wife, because she was barren . . . and Rebekah . . . conceived" (Gen. 25:21). With regard to Rachel we are told "and God hearkened to her" (30:22), presumably because she had prayed. Hannah beseeched God for a "man child" (1 Sam. 1:11). An unnamed woman cried "Your servant was barren and had no child, though I lived with my husband thirty years. And every hour and every day during those thirty years I besought the Most High, night and day" (2 Esd. 9:43).

It is not recorded that Sarah prayed to relieve her sterility, but the narrative mentions that a messenger of God promised her a son. Being post-menopausal, she laughed derisively . . . "Now Abraham and Sarah were old and well stricken in age; and it had ceased to be with Sarah after the manner of women. Therefore Sarah laughed . . ." (Gen. 18:11–12). Abraham had similar sentiments "Then Abraham . . . laughed, and said . . . Shall a child be born unto him that is an hundred years old, and shall Sarah, that is ninety years old, bear?" (17:17).

One other post-menopausal conception is recorded in the Bible: "Elisabeth . . . hath also conceived a son in her old age . . ." (Luke 1:36). While this extract is not conclusive, the succeeding phrase makes it almost certain that the "old age" meant "after the time when it is normally possible for a woman to conceive"—"For with God nothing shall be impossible" (1:37).

The Hebrew view of conception was simple: The male provided the "seed" and the female provided the womb—the fertile soil wherein Yahweh worked the miracle of growth. They had no knowledge of the part played by the ovum; and equally so, of course, had no idea of the part played by the sperm. But they believed, and indeed it was reasonable to assume, that a man who was capable of producing semen, was able, with the help of God, to beget children. As a matter of interest it may be noted that both the Talmud and the Koran consider that the seminal fluid originated in the head and reached the testicles via the spinal column. Presumably the biblical Hebrews entertained similar misconceptions. Clearly they knew nothing of male sterility in those possessed of ostensibly normal organs, and, notwithstanding Deut. 7:14 (azoospermia?), barrenness was always blamed on the woman—through the agency of God.

Of Hannah it is stated that "the Lord has shut up her womb" (1 Sam. 1:5). Sarah complained that "the Lord hath restrained me from bearing" (Gen. 16:2), and God is given the credit for "opening the womb" of Leah (29:31) and of Rachel (30:22). The prophet threatens Ephraim's family with sterility (Hos. 9:11). Because of a misdemeanor "Therefore Michal . . . had no child unto the day of her death" (2 Sam. 6:23). God's prescribed punishment for an illicit union is sterility in the partners (Lev. 20:20–21), and the punishment for King Abimelech's attempt at seduction was God's curse "Behold, thou art but a dead man" (Gen. 20:3), i.e. a man whose seed would not be fruitful; and indeed "the Lord had fast closed up all the wombs of the house of Abimelech" (20:18), but after suitable prayer "God healed Abimelech, and his wife, and his maidservants; and they bare children" (20:17).

### Ungodly Influences in Pregnancy

The singular purpose of the biblical editors in expurgating all reference to idolatry, is responsible for the remarkable lack of discussion concerning charms, symbols, pilgrimages and incantations for facilitating pregnancy. To God alone was ascribed cause and effect; yet the known universality of pagan aids to conception makes it difficult to believe that the Hebrews did not practise them to some extent. A number of passages are illuminating in this respect:

Firstly there is the curious story of the mandrakes referred to in Gen. 30:14. Egyptian notions connected these roots with fructifying properties, understandable when it is noted that this plant often consists of twin extremities meeting superiorly in a rounded belly. Babylonians imputed sedative qualities to the mandragora, these being not far removed from Egyptian notions because tense, worried women, obsessed with the desire for pregnancy, may be thwarted in this aim unless they are relaxed and soothed into a state of contentment, more conducive to pregnancy; and it is in this respect that mandragora may act as a catalyst for pregnancy to take place.

Rachel, long sterile, bargained for and acquired the precious mandrakes. But there the tale ends abruptly. There is no sequel to the story of the mandrakes. Probably in the original version of the tale, Rachel conceived with their aid, but the later editors of the narrative saw herein a heathen superstition, hence this portion was expurgated and a more seemly phrase substituted: "God . . . opened her womb" (30:22)

Then there is the matter of the *teraphim* (a plural noun), these being images, household gods, which Rachel stole from her father (Gen. 31:19,30, see also 35:2–4). Whatever their value to the head of a household (tokens of legitimate inheritance of property?), for women they were fertility amulets associated with the cult of the mother goddess and used as charms to secure the increase of man. Michal, wife of David, also owned an image (1 Sam. 19:13). Interestingly enough, she was sterile, so that her possession of an image is understandable.

The god Baal is referred to numerous times in the Bible. His helpmeet was Ashtoreth, and both of these were the local gods of fertility, male and female. Ashtoreth is referred to in Judg. 2:13 and 10:6. Solomon set up a temple for her in order to please his Phoenician wife (1 Kings 11:5,8). She was the great Mother Goddess of the Near East, and was called Ishtar in Babylon, Ashtart by the Phoenicians and Astarte by the Greeks. Another goddess, perhaps with fructifying power, was Asherah (Deut. 7:5, 12:3, 16:21) who is falsely translated as "groves" in the Authorized Version. The Asherah was a wooden pole (cut down by Gideon: Judg. 6:25) which was originally a sacred tree of heathen worship, and represented a female divinity.

A Jewish tradition adds to the story of Manoah's wife in Judg. 13 an account of a recipe given her by her neighbors to promote conception—as a result of which she became the mother of Samson.

### *Marital Aberrations*

Biblical legends have suggested that the story of the pregnancy of Lot's daughters (Gen. 19:31–38) indicates their artificial insemination by their father's semen—produced by stimulation during a drunken stupor; but it seems more likely that after making him drunk, they actually had incestuous unions with him.

The apocryphal writer ben Sira (about 150 B.C.E.) is rumored to have been born following artificial insemination. His mother entered a warm bath soon after it had been vacated by her own father, and there received his seed. The son of this conception was called ben Zera (son of seed), but when he grew up and understood the significance of his name, he was ashamed, and changed it to ben Sira.

There is a Biblical reference to a man practising contraception. According to Law, Onan married his deceased brother's wife (Levirate marriage), but practised coitus interruptus—perhaps even because he intended to deny offspring to his brother. "And Onan knew that the seed should not be his; and it came to pass . . . that he spilled it on the ground" (Gen. 38:9). We can understand from what has been written on the necessity and value of children, that coitus interruptus was a heinous offence against man and God, and for practising it, Onan was struck dead. The Bible mentions that the husband, Er, had also been slain by the Lord, and Hebrew commentary favors the view that he was executed for the selfsame crime.

In later centuries schismatic sects of Jews deemed it a

virtue to practise continence, a view shared as well by many early Christian sects, and given great impetus and support by several early Christian writers and by the examples of Christ and Paul, both celibates. The first commandment of God to man had been "Be fruitful and multiply" (Gen. 1:28) and the asceticism and sexual abstention as practised by some (but not all) of the Jewish Essene sects and by Christian sects anticipating the early return of their messiah, was certainly not in keeping with traditional Hebrew views on the importance of children. In biblical Hebrew there is no word for bachelor.

## *Childbirth*

Childbirth begins with impregnation. Within the female generative organs, within the nutritive womb, the semen congealed to form an embryo. The earliest phase of conception is noted thus: "My substance was not hid from thee, when I was made in secret . . . My undeveloped substance (*golem,* Hebrew) did thy eyes see" (Ps. 139:15,16). The *golem* is an amorphous mass, the earliest stage in the development of the embryo. It is fabled that Adam was a *golem,* a lump of clay, for three hours, after which his nostrils received the breath of life. The Psalmist describes the mystery of conception with awe: "I will praise thee: for I am fearfully and wonderfully made" (Ps. 139:14). Job's opinion on embryogenesis is as follows: "Like milk didst thou pour me out, and like cheese didst thou curdle me. With skin and flesh didst thou clothe me, and with bone and sinews didst thou cover me" (10:10,11).

The wise author of Ecclesiastes professes ignorance of the whole matter: "thou knowest not . . . how the bones do grow in the womb of her that is with child" (11:5). With continued growth "quickening" or the movement of the fetus *in utero,* may be felt by the mother. This is recorded in the pregnancy of Rebekah (Gen. 25) and in the gestation described in Luke 1:41: at six months, Elisabeth's babe "leaped in her womb." Some three months after impregnation pregnancy was clinically recognizable (Gen. 38:24).

Among the ancients the belief in maternal impression during pregnancy was widespread, and, indeed, is not unknown today. The story of Jacob and the speckled sheep (Gen. 30) evidences this belief.

Pregnancy is so important an occurrence that it would be surprising if the gods were not credited with having "a hand in it." It has already been noted that the God of Israel could "open" and "shut" wombs. Some deities could do even better; they could induce pregnancy, though in such cases the role of the man remained in some doubt. Until well after the Christian era, Egyptians, Mesopotamians, Greeks, Romans and perhaps Jews believed that conception was possible without human masculine intervention. Jesus was born of the Holy Ghost (Matt. 1:18,20) and a virgin mother (Matt. 1:23); certainly a pagan, not a Jewish idea, and in any event one based on a determined and willful mistranslation of the Hebrew word *almah* (Isa. 7:14) and also of the Septuagint's equivalent, *parthenos,* which does not necessarily connote virginity.

Other famous men giving credit to gods for their conception include Buddha, some of the pharaohs, Julius Caesar, Alexander the Great, Augustus, Cyrus, and scores of lesser lights.

It is difficult to determine exactly how much influence these worthies apportioned to their various gods for their alleged induction of conception. It is possible to take a kindly view and suggest that the deity was given remote credit, while the masculine factor was fully appreciated as being of immediate importance. Queen Hatshepsut, a remarkable woman of the 18th dynasty in Egypt, knew very well that she was the offspring of her father Thothmes 1 and her mother Aahmes, but nevertheless held herself as having been engendered by the god Amon in the figure of her mortal father, doubtless in order to bolster her claim to the throne. Nebuchadnezzar described himself thus: "I am Nebuchadnezzar . . . the firstborn son of Nabopolassar, King of Babel am I. Since Bel had created me, the goddess Erua and the god Marduk had formed my figure in the womb . . ." He mentions his father as a human person, while at the same time also giving credit to three of his favorite gods. This is not far removed from the Psalmist's admission ". . . thou art he that took me out of the womb . . . thou art my God from my mother's belly" (22:9,10), or from the view of 2 Esd. 8:8 ". . . thou dost give life to the body which is now fashioned in the womb."

## Prenatal Care

As regards prenatal care, we know only that in the two recorded instances of twin birth, both were diagnosed antepartum, the first by God: "And the Lord said unto her, Two nations are in thy womb . . ." (Gen. 25:23), a diagnosis fully corroborated, for, "And when her days to be delivered were fulfilled, behold, there were twins in her womb" (25:24). The other diagnosis was made by a midwife, who was so certain of the presence of twins, that when a hand presented, she tied a scarlet thread about it (Gen. 38:28) in order to establish primogeniture.

Prenatal advice in the matter of diet was given by an angel to the wife of Manoah: "And the angel of the Lord . . . said . . . thou shalt conceive, and bear a son. Now therefore beware . . . and drink not wine nor strong drink, and eat not any unclean thing" (Judg. 13:3,4).

Some more comments on mandrakes in labor may be in order. The mandragora was known in Babylonia since the earliest recorded times, but was not known in Egypt until Ptolemaic times (about 330 B.C.E.) so that any Hebrew ideas on this plant were presumably similar to those entertained by the Mesopotamians. Now although the Egyptians linked mandrakes with sexual and aphrodisiac properties, the Babylonians considered them primarily anodynes and soporifics; and this conception has generally prevailed through the centuries:

> Not poppy nor mandragora,
> Nor all the drowsy syrups of the world,
> Shall ever medicine thee to that sweet sleep
> Which thou ow'dst yesterday.
>
> Othello 3:3

It is possible therefore that Rachel's bargaining for the mandrakes (Gen. 30:14) may have indicated that she was already pregnant, indeed, near to term, and wanted them to ease the expected pains of a first labor.

### Normal Labor

Normal labor is recorded among women having their first infant and also among multiparae. Apparently grande multiparity was unusual, though it is noted that a womb may bear 10 children, one after the other, never 10 at once (2 Esd. 5:46,47). Many households had numerous wives (Solomon had 1,000—1 Kings 11:3) and hordes of children (Rehoboam had 88 children, but hardly did his wives justice: he had 78 of them—2 Chron. 11:21); yet the individual mother seldom had more than 7 children (1 Sam. 2:5, Jer. 15:9). Possibly this was due to the relative infertility associated with very prolonged lactation.

Normal labor at full term is recorded briefly according to a standard pattern. "Sarah conceived, and bare . . . a son . . . at the set time" (Gen. 21:2). Rebekah travailed "when her days to be delivered were fulfilled . . ." (Gen. 25:24). "Now Elisabeth's full time came that she should be delivered" (Luke 1:57). Of Mary: "And so it was that . . . the days were accomplished that she should be delivered" (Luke 2:6).

Genesis 3:16 implies that labor was originally meant to be a painless procedure, but as a result of "The Fall" God decreed that "in sorrow" (toil? labor?) "thou shalt bring forth children." There is a fable that Jochebed, the mother of Moses, having led a blameless life, was not subject to the Curse of Eve, and had no distress with her deliveries.

The travail of labor is remarked upon several times (1 Sam. 4:19, Gen. 38:27, Jer. 22:23, 30:6, 31:8, 50:43, Mic. 4:10, 5:3, Hos. 13:13, Isa. 13:8, 21:3, 26:17, 42:14, John 16:21, 1 Thess. 5:3, Rev. 12:2, Sira 48:19, 2 Esd. 4:42, 10:12) and the intensity of the second stage is evidently referred to specifically "a woman with child, in the ninth month, when the time of her delivery draws near, has great pains about her womb for two or three hours beforehand" (2 Esd. 16:38). That labor was more painful in primiparae was also noted: "For I have heard a voice as of a woman in travail, and the anguish as of her that bringeth forth her first child" (Jer. 4:31). Jeremiah also portrays the pain and fear of women in labor: "And the heart of the mighty men of Moab at that day shall be as the heart of a woman in her pangs" (48:41, 49:22, 24). The apocryphal author of 2 Esdras remarks that "the ways of entering this world were made narrow, grievous and toilsome . . . full of dangers and burdened with great hardships" (7:11,12), while Tobias reminds us "Thou shalt honor thy mother all the days of her life: For thou must be mindful of the perils she suffered for thee in her womb" (Tobit 4:4).

Contrariwise, some labors might have been unusually easy: "And the midwives said unto Pharaoh, Because the Hebrew women are not as the Egyptian women; for they are lively, and are delivered ere the midwives come in unto them" (Exod. 1:19). It seems that they had easy rapid labors without the assistance of midwives, or more probably these latter were making up excuses to explain their failure to report the birth of male infants among the Hebrews.

Physicians in ancient Egypt, as in the whole of the ancient world, did not practise obstetrics, but left this entirely to midwives. However, the attention of a regular midwife was probably exceptional; their service is indicated but once during the Hebrew sojourn in Egypt (Exod. 1:15) and twice more in Genesis: the assistance of midwives is recorded in the parturition of Rachel (35:17) and of Tamar (38:28). Most births were attended by friends, by experienced multiparae, and by what are loosely called "nurses," these being attendants who probably doubled as "home helps." Wealthy households doubtless had a "nurse" or a "lady-in-waiting" to care for the mistress: "And they sent away Rebekah their sister, and her nurse" (Gen. 24:59). Friends delivered Ruth ". . . and she bare a son. And the *woman* said unto Naomi . . ." (Ruth 4:13,14). When the wife of Phineas travailed "the *women* that stood by her said . . . thou hast born a son" (1 Sam. 4:20).

Women in childbirth crouched on a bed or birthstool, their bodies in a vertical position. One midwife sat behind and clasped her round the body during the pains of labor while another knelt in front ready to receive the infant. The necessity for two midwives to minister to a laboring woman is probably reflected in the mention of two midwives (Shifrah and Puah) in Exod. 1:15. Their names give us no extra

*113*

obstetrical information. It has been suggested that Shifrah means "beauty" and that Puah is related to an Ugaritic word meaning "freeborn girl of marriageable age, but still living in her father's house." It occurs as a proper name in Ugarit.[1]

There is a legend that at the birth of Jesus three male priests actually rendered obstetric assistance. The term "magi" is early Persian for a Zoroastrian priest.

The method of labor was that of squatting, practised by primitive people to this day. The accoucher crouched beneath the parturient woman, and delivered the baby on her lap. It seems that Rachel delivered her maid of the child that she was to keep as her own: "And she (Rachel) said, Behold my maid Bilhah, go in unto her; and she shall bear upon my knees" (Gen. 30:3). However, this phrase is probably figurative, and the same applies to "the children . . . (who) . . . were brought up upon Joseph's knees" (50:23).

It is likely that men absented themselves during delivery: "Cursed be the man who brought tidings to my father, saying, a man child is born unto thee" (Jer. 20:15). In Ugaritic (Canaanite) literature, it is also noted that a father absented himself during delivery.[1]

Presumably women labored in their huts, though affluent Egyptian women had access to "lying-in" homes. Apparently Jesus was born in a house (Matt. 2:11). At least some deliveries took place in the open: "I raised thee up under the apple tree: there my mother brought thee forth: there she brought thee forth that bare thee" (Song of Sol. 8:5). Deliveries outside of the house or tent (still a common practice among present-day Beduin) certainly carried less risk of sepsis.

Reference to Egyptian hieroglyphics indicates that cephalic presentation was the rule. The hieroglyph for "to give birth to" was a picture of a squatting woman with the fetal head emerging from the perineum.

### Birthstools

Obstetric chairs must have been in widespread use: "And he (pharaoh) said, When ye do the office of a midwife . . . and see them upon the stools . . ." (Exod. 1:16). Birthstools were used in Europe until the 18th century and in the Middle East to this very day.

In Hebrew the obstetric stools are called *ovnaim,* a term which is neither singular nor plural but dual. The Egyptians also rendered some nouns in the dual form until about 1300 B.C.E. The obstetric chair consisted of two stones (*ovnaim*) over which parturient women delivered. After about 1300 B.C.E. the Egyptian language dropped the dual number and called it "the brick," or "the brick of bearing," and this coincided with the introduction of an additional stone uniting the two into one structure, so that instead of two parallel bricks, thus: II, the addition of a posterior cross-bar united them to form a single seat, thus: U.

A parturient woman could adopt two methods of delivering "on the stools." When two separate bricks were used, it was customary for the woman to sit on her haunches, her knees resting on the clay bricks, and her feet on the ground, while the buttocks rested on her heels. A midwife then supported her trunk while a second waited in front of the bricks, ready to receive the infant. In Persia women delivered on two bricks, as described above, and probably also in Babylonia. Hippocrates (about 450 B.C.E.) used an obstetric chair. A bas-relief from Ptolemaic times (after 300 B.C.E.) shows a woman delivering on two bricks.

With the introduction of a third brick and the unification into a single structure, it is likely that women ceased sitting on their haunches, and instead, actually sat on the stool itself.

The rabbis have considered that pharaoh's command need not be translated "When ye see them upon the stools (*ovnaim*) . . ." but as "When ye see by the *ovnaim*" (two stones, i.e. testes) "that it is a boy . . ." But though ingenious, it is probably not the correct interpretation. Hebrew commentators feel that it is more likely that *ovnaim* refer to the two stones of the parturition chair, and not to the "two stones" in the scrotum.

Old statuettes from Peru, and also from as near as Cyprus, illustrate another primitive method of parturition: one that it is very tempting to think may also have been practised by the Hebrews or by their even more primitive antecedants. It is also a method from which the obstetric chair might conceivably have been derived. The parturient woman sits on the lap of an assistant (her husband or a midwife) who supports her from behind. This would make an interesting basis for Rachel's suggestion: "Behold my maid Bilhah, go in unto her; and she shall bear upon my knees" (Gen. 30:3). The same applies to "the children . . . (who) . . . were brought up upon Joseph's knees" (50:23), and to the "knees which received" Job (3:12).

## Obstetric Complications

Luke 2:5 observes that Mary was "great with child." There is a temptation to draw an inference that the physician Luke was being clinically perceptive and noting an instance of hydramnios. However, this is not so, for the Greek version of this passage says nothing about "great with child," but merely has the equivalent of "pregnant." Moreover it is most unlikely that the physician Luke (Col. 4:14) was the same individual as the Luke who penned the gospel.

The only record of abnormal presentation is that of the

hand presentation among the twins born to Tamar. The subsequent progress of the birth is interesting: "the one put out his hand: and the midwife took and bound upon his hand a scarlet thread (but) . . . he drew back his hand (and) . . . his brother came out" (Gen. 38:28,29). Tamar must have had an unusually roomy pelvis for the twins to maneuver so easily. During birth her perineum was probably torn by Pharez ("to burst out") who probably underwent something of a precipitate delivery. Another presumptive hand presentation is that of Jacob who, following Esau, had his hand clasped on Esau's heel (Gen. 25:26).

Breech delivery is not noted clearly, although it may perhaps be inferred from the description of the parturition of Rachel: "And it came to pass, when she (Rachel) was in hard labour, that the midwife said unto her, Fear not; for this also is a son for thee . . . And Rachel died" (Gen. 35:17–19).

The point to note is that the midwife was able to identify the child as a son while she was still in hard labor, so presumably the breech was presenting. That being so, it is tempting to postulate that her death was somehow connected with maternal conditions commonly associated with the occurrence of breech presentation. Perhaps she had a placenta previa and suffered antepartum hemorrhage—possibly precipitated by the roughness of the journey on which she was engaged at the time. Being "bled out," the postpartum loss acted as "the straw to break the camel's back." It is unlikely that there was any form of disproportion as the child apparently suffered no injury; moreover we may perhaps infer that the infant was somewhat premature, for it is not noted that "her days to be delivered were fulfilled." It is also worthy of note that the long journey might have precipitated premature delivery, although the fact that a midwife was at hand would possibly indicate that in any event her time was near. Possibly she died of antepartum and postpartum hemorrhage.

The only other record of maternal death is that of the wife of Phineas, who travailed in premature labor: "And about the time of her death, the women that stood by her said . . . thou hast born a son. But she answered not" (1 Sam. 4:20). Presumably she also died of postpartum hemorrhage although eclamptic convulsions and toxemia are also possible.

There are but two records of multiple birth—the twins born to Rebekah (Gen. 25:24) and to Tamar (38:27). Triplets are not noted in the Bible although the Egyptian Westcar Papyrus notes their occurrence. Hebrew commentary and tradition declare that Eve did not bear Cain alone, or Abel. Cain is thought to have been one of twins, and Abel one of triplets. Eve is then believed to have been extraordinarily prolific, both in the number of her subsequent pregnancies, and in the number of infants born at each parturition. A similar legend concerns the sons born to Jacob. All of them (except Joseph) were one of twins, the other being a girl. The twin pregnancy of the first-born, Reuben, lasted but seven months.[2] Thomas (Didymus: John 20:24) was probably one of twins; his name is derived from the Hebrew *tomim*—twins.

Siamese twinning has been considered in the first chapter: Adam and Eve were believed to have been joined together prior to their famous operation. The oriental conception of the first humans as being androgynous is also to be found in Plato (Symposion) and in Rabbinic literature (Bereshit R.8, Wayiqra R.14, Erubin 18a, Berakhoth 61a).

The birth of monsters is recorded in 2 Esd. 5:8, their occurrence being linked with the consequences of cohabitation during the menses.

Uterine inertia is described in identical passages in 2 Kings 19:3 and Isa. 37:3 ". . . for the children are come to the birth, and there is not strength to bring forth." Neither Caesarian section nor the piecemeal removal of a dead fetus are noted in the Bible, although they are mentioned in the Talmud (Arakin 7, Ohalot 7:6).

Premature labor is also described. In the case of the twins born to Tamar, the evidence is presumptive, and entirely a matter of semantics. Whereas with the twins of Rebekah it is written "And her days to be delivered were fulfilled . . ." (Gen. 25:24), in the same manner as the full term pregnancies of others similarly described, with Tamar's twins it is but written "And it came to pass in the time of her travail . . ." (38:27). Possibly her "days to be delivered" had not been fulfilled.

The premature labor of Phineas' wife is clearly described, and followed immediately upon hearing disastrous personal news: "Phineas' wife was with child, near to be delivered: and when she heard the tidings . . . she bowed herself and travailed . . ." (1 Sam. 4:19).

Some commentators feel that Moses was a premature baby, born as early as 28 or 30 weeks gestation. His prematurity is only just hinted at: we read that "the woman conceived, and bare a son" (Exod. 2:2). We are not told that this occurred "when her days to be delivered were fulfilled." As in the case of Tamar, this is but a semantic surmise, but is greatly strengthened by the ensuing phrase "and when she saw him that he was a goodly child . . ." (2:2). This apparent inspection of a newborn infant is unprecedented, and therefore significant. After examining him his mother decided that he was viable ("goodly," "beautiful," cf. "The Torah," 1962. Jewish Publication Society of America) for "she hid him three months" (2:2). Her reason for hiding him was simple. Pharaoh had ordered that all newly born Hebrew infants were to be drowned. Now she was known to be pregnant, and would have been expecting the Egyptian authorities to be visiting her at full term, so that until that time she could safely hide him. But, as the hazardous time drew near "when she could not longer hide him, she took for him an ark of bulrushes . . ." (2:3), and hid him at the water's edge.

However, it must be stated that the biblical evidence for his prematurity is tenuous and is entirely a matter of semantics and hair splitting: "goodly" may refer not to viability, but to his good nature. Being a contented infant, he did not cry, but lay quietly, so that his mother could safely hide him at home for a time.

There is a legend that in the idyllic period preceding the flood, all pregnancies ended prematurely. Children were born fully mature after but a few days gestation. So mature were they in fact, that they could assist with severing the umbilical cord, and could walk and talk.[2]

Postmaturity is not recorded in the Bible although we can be sure that some inquiring minds had entertained the possibility of postmaturity in antiquity; "So he answered me and said, Go thy way to a woman with child, and ask of her when she hath fulfilled her nine months, if the womb may keep the birth any longer within her. Then said I, no, Lord, that it can not" (2 Esd. 4:40–41).

There is but one instance of death in early neonatal life (1 Kings 3:19) but no actual instance of stillbirth or miscarriage. Yet their occurrence was well-known and annotated. However, procured abortion is quite unknown in the scriptures. The prophet recognizes neonatal death: "There shall be no more thence an infant of days . . . for the child shall die an hundred years old" (Isa. 65:20).

Miscarriage is considered a divine judgement: "Give them a miscarrying womb" thunders the prophet (Hos.

9:14). "Let . . . them pass away" cries the Psalmist, "like the untimely birth of a woman" (58:8). God promises the Hebrews that he "will take sickness away . . . There shall nothing cast their young" (Exod. 23:25–26). The Mosaic law mentions the possibility of miscarriage: "If men strive, and hurt a woman with child, so that her fruit depart from her . . ." (Exod. 21:22). Job writes of miscarriage as "hidden untimely birth . . . infants which never saw light" (3:16). The Hebrew word here used (*nefel*) rendered "untimely birth" actually means, and can equally well be translated as "miscarriage" since it indicates "falling"—that is, falling (prematurely) out of the womb.

"Why died I not from the womb?" Job also complains, "why did I not give up the ghost when I came out of the belly?" (3:11). The complaint is echoed in 2 Esd. 5:35 "Why then was I born . . . why did not my mother's womb become my grave?", sentiments which conjure up visions of missed abortion and lithopedion. The same author writes that "women with child will bring forth untimely infants at three or four months . . ." (6:21), but he is clearly mistaken in the matter of viability for he adds "and they shall live and dance" (6:22).

There is a legend that Hagar had an abortion. When she conceived and became haughty, her mistress Sarah was envious and gazed at her with an Evil Eye, as a result of which her pregnancy miscarried.[2] Only subsequently did she become pregnant with Ishmael.

There is a good description of a macerated fetus in Num. 12:12 "Let her not be as one dead, of whom the flesh is half consumed when he cometh out of his mother's womb." It has been suggested that Sarah's long-standing sterility was due to Rh incompatibility and that she only conceived and delivered Isaac (homozygous Rh negative) after having repeated miscarriages.

It has also been suggested that Erb's palsy was common among the tribe of Benjamin[3] but this form of paralysis has been confused with what is clearly ambidexterity (Judg. 20:15–16, 1 Chron. 12:2).

## The Placenta

Of the third stage of labor we know very little. The placenta (*shilya*—Hebrew) is mentioned in some biblical translations (e.g. Moffat's, "The Torah," Jewish Publication Society of America, 1962) in Deut. 28: 57, while in others it is incorrectly rendered as "the young one" (*shilya*) "between her legs."

Cutting of the umbilical cord is noted in Ezek. 16:4. Presumably a flint knife was used, and the cord ligated thereafter. If we can judge from the recognition of a "caul of the heart" in Hos. 13:8, we may hazard the guess that an obstetric caul (chorio-amniotic membranes) was also recognized. This caul may be intended by an oblique reference in Ps. 139:13 ". . . thou hast covered me in my mother's womb."

A "lying-in" period is not described, but a woman was considered ritually unclean for 33 days after the delivery of a boy, and 66 days in the case of a girl, after which she was acceptable once more for all activities, sacred and profane. Though primarily ritual, this isolation of the woman during the puerperium must have had a sanitary value.

The placenta is also mentioned indirectly with reference to the life of David, indicating that the Hebrew writings of this period had an animistic conception of the soul similar to that entertained by their Egyptian neighbors. Both viewed the placenta as a container of a portion of the spirit, regarding it as an embodiment of the external soul. The placenta —preserved as a "bundle of life"—was a talisman for the preservation of good fortune and had a special affinity with the individual it had nourished in the womb; so much so, that it still contained a portion of his spirit.

These remarks make intelligible the statement of the woman Abigail to the fugitive David: "Yet a man is risen to pursue thee, and to seek thy soul: but the soul of my lord shall be bound in the *bundle of life* with the Lord thy God; and the souls of thine enemies, them shall he sling out, as out of the middle of a sling" (1 Sam. 25:29).

## Conspicuous Absences

In the varied narratives of the many facets of human experience as narrated in the Bible, there are perhaps two conditions associated with childbirth of which one might have expected to see mention—since they were not unknown among other primitive cultures.

Firstly there is the matter of *vagitus uterinus,* the crying of an infant *in utero.* Mere quickening, or the movement of a fetus *in utero,* is recorded in the pregnancy of Rebekah (Gen. 25) and also in the gestation of Elisabeth (Luke 1.41) whose baby "leaped in her womb." But *vagitus uterinus* is noted only in legend. Its occurrence is mentioned in the text of some of the writings found among the ruins of Ashurbanipal's (7th century B.C.E.) palace in Nineveh. Zoroaster is said to have laughed in his mother's womb. Mahomet cried therein. At his birth, Noah opened his mouth and praised the Lord. When Moses was not yet a day old he could walk and talk; indeed, he refused his mother's milk. Exactly the same fable is related of the apocryphal writer ben Sira, who refused his mother's milk and demanded solid food instead. Jesus spoke to his mother immediately after birth; so did Buddha.

In the period prior to the Flood, children were born after but a few days gestation, and immediately after birth they could walk and talk and even aided their mothers to sever the umbilical cord. When Cain was born, he immediately ran off and returned holding in his hands a shaft of reed.[2] Hence his name (*Cain*: reed—Hebrew).

Abraham is also the subject of a precocity legend. His mother, Emtelai, bore him in secret in a cave because King Nimrod, warned by his astrologers that a usurper was shortly to be born, ordered all male newborns to be destroyed. His mother placed him within a cave, trusting that God would care for him. The angel Gabriel made milk to flow from his right little finger, and Abraham sucked on it for ten days, growing rapidly, walking and talking. When his mother returned 20 days after the birth to note his progress, she found a grown man.[2]

The second matter is the curious condition of couvade—the vicarious travail of a man while his wife is in labor. Couvade was not uncommon in antiquity, and even to this day is practised in Indonesia, Burma and parts of South America. In Brazil, an Indian woman may get up immediately after childbirth while the father goes to bed with the newborn baby and gets all the congratulations and felicitations of friends and relatives while the mother is more or less ignored.

The reason for this procedure is one that the Hebrews would have understood immediately, for they had the same views: that conception is entirely dependent upon the male, the women's role being quite passive: she only hatches the egg, so to speak. Hence, once the baby is born, the father has the only close relationship to the infant and can take his newborn to bed with him. The mother's function—the use of her womb—is over.

## *Feeding*

It may be taken for granted that the apocryphal mother who remarked ". . . I brought (my son) up with much care" (2 Esd. 9:46) included prolonged breast feeding as part of that care.

In various parts of the ancient world, superstitions about nursing included a view that the initial colostrum was unsuitable for infants, so that for the first few hours or days of life a wet nurse might have been substituted. To what extent such conceptions were extant in Israel it is impossible to say.

The role of the breasts was clear: ". . . And when the womb gives up again what has been created in it, thou hast commanded that . . . milk should be supplied which is the fruit of the breasts, so that what has been fashioned may be nourished for a time . . ." (2 Esd. 8:9–11). The scriptures are clear that it was normal for Hebrew mothers to breast feed their infants. Not only was it a normal function, but it was in fact a duty. In postbiblical years the Law actually forbade a widow's remarriage before her sucking infant had reached the age of two years, lest a new courtship lead to neglect of the child. There is a suggestion that nursing was a source of satisfaction and emotional solidarity between mother and child: "Can a mother forget her sucking child, that she should not have compassion on the son of her womb?" (Isa. 49:15).

Breast feeding continued for a period of two or three years, normally decreasing slowly and being finally ended when the last deciduous teeth appeared. At this time a child was considered "grown." Nursing was prolonged not only because of its intimate relation to dentition, but also because it was considered that it was part of good care in the nurture of the child, and that premature weaning was tantamount to neglect. The Koran requires (where possible) nursing for a number of years (2:223, 46:15, 31:14). It is also probable that the ancients considered that prolonged lactation decreased the chances of conception, and this view is probably illustrated by Hos. 1:8 "Now when she had weaned (her daughter) she conceived and bare a son." This passage can be interpreted to mean that the second conception could not occur until weaning was completed, and in fact she might even have weaned her daughter somewhat prematurely in order to become pregnant with a son.

## Wet Nursing

If for any reason a mother could not breast feed her baby, then wet nursing was resorted to, a procedure still in vogue in some parts of the western world. Evidently failure of lactation was not uncommon, for wet nursing was well established in antiquity. There were wet nurses in the homes of Greek aristocracy at the time of Homer (7th century B.C.E.), and like some of the biblical nurses to be noted, these probably grew up in the household to become nanny, tutor, and perhaps later—accoucher. In Mesopotamia wet nursing was normally carried on for three years. The Code of Hammurabi (1700 B.C.E.) in Babylonia ruled that if a wet nurse had a sucking infant die, and in taking on another infant, failed to inform the parents that she "had lost a previous case" then she was to be punished by having one of her breasts amputated.

In Egypt the nobility were known to have employed wet nurses who were engaged on contract to breast feed for six months, permitting cow's milk thereafter. The hieroglyphic designation of a wet nurse was a picture of a breast.

Failure of lactation is hinted at in the curse of Hosea:

"give them . . . dry breasts" (9:14), and the author of Lamentation notes "Even the sea monsters draw out the breast, they give suck to their young ones . . . The tongue of the sucking child cleaveth to the roof of his mouth for thirst" (4:3–4). This last phrase is open to two interpretations: it does not necessarily follow that the thirst is due to failure of lactation; the nursling might be thirsty for lack of access to a breast, or lack of water.

Moses, legendarily premature, was breast fed by his mother for the three months that he was hidden at home, and thereafter, by means of a subterfuge, she continued as his wet nurse. In the Koran this stratagem has the variant that Egyptian wet nurses were first offered and rejected (28:2) which may be interpreted as meaning that Mahomet considered that maternal milk strengthened family and racial characteristics in a child.

Apparently Tahpenes, Queen of Egypt, nursed her nephew Genubath. Presumably his own mother could not: "And the sister of Tahpenes bare . . . Genubath . . . whom Tahpenes weaned in Pharaoh's house . . ." (1 Kings 11:20). Alternatively, this statement could also mean that Tahpenes merely organized the weaning ceremony in the palace, and that his mother did in fact nurse him.

The English term "nurse" is used rather loosely in the Authorized Version, covering two distinct Hebrew terms: *meneket* (wet nurse) and *omenet* (guardian, nanny, tutor). When the sister of Moses asked "Shall I . . . call . . . a nurse . . . that she may nurse the child?" (Exod. 2:7) she was referring to a *meneket,* a wet nurse. In 2 Kings 11:2 we learn that "they hid him (the boy Joash) . . . and his nurse."—again a wet nurse; presumably Joash was under three years of age at the time. On the other hand, a wet nurse accompanied Rebekah (Gen. 24:59) when she was already an adult. Presumably her function had now changed to that of an attendant, although as a loyal past wet nurse, she remained on to serve this aristocratic family.

Egyptian hieroglyphs also shed light on this distinction. The hieroglyphic picture of a female breast had two meanings: it might refer to a *mnd* (vowels unknown), this being a breast itself, male or female, or the hieroglyph might refer to a *mnkt*—a wet nurse, this same word *mnkt* being also used to indicate a milking cow. Interestingly enough, a related verb meant "to educate"; perhaps the ancients felt that education began with breast feeding.[1] A lactating camel is also called a *meneket* (Gen. 32:15), a milch camel.

Mephibosheth, of royal blood (2 Sam. 4:4), at the age of five years was taken up, understandably enough, not by a wet nurse, but by a nanny (*omenet*), and the reference in Ruth 4:16 to the effect that "Naomi took the child" (Ruth's infant) "and laid it in her bosom, and became nurse unto it" refers not to a wet nurse, but to an *omenet,* a nanny. "And kings shall be thy nursing fathers" (Isa. 49:23) refers to the function of a guardian, while "and queens thy nursing mothers" refers to wet nursing. Num. 11:12 also refers to nursing fathers: "Have I conceived all this people? Have I begotten them, that thou shoulds't say unto me, Carry them in thy bosom, as a nursing father beareth the sucking child?" —again, the "nursing father" here refers only to the function of guardianship. The same holds true for the relationship of Mordechai to his niece Esther (Esther 2:7). The statement in Job 21:24 "His breasts are full of milk" is no affirmation of male lactaticn, but is a tenuous interpretation of a difficult and doubtful passage. It is just as easily rendered "His loins" (meaning testes) "are full of semen." A nurse could have great affection for her charges (1 Thess. 2:7). Wet nurses are also mentioned in 2 Esd. 2:25.

Though there is no mention of the subject, the ancient

Hebrews doubtless had their methods (as did the Greeks) of judging the fitness of a nurse to suckle, and of the quality of her milk.

### Artificial Feeding

Abel was a keeper of sheep (Gen. 4:2). The milk of animals was available for adult use (Judg. 4:19), and might also have been given to babies. In Egypt, cow's milk was given to babies after the age of six months and in the 7th century B.C.E. King Ashurbanipal of Assyria, while yet an infant, was given cow's milk. In the mountainous territory of central Canaan however, cow's milk must have been scarce, though it is mentioned (Isa. 7:21–22, Deut. 32:14). Most milk used was that of sheep, goats and milch camels (Gen 32·15) That any infant was ever brought up wholly on animal's milk from birth, is very doubtful. Milk is coupled with honey in Gen. 3:8.

The containers, the infant feeding bottles of biblical times, were made of clay. Such are known to have been used in Egypt, Cyprus, Canaan and elsewhere. Possibly vegetable shells and suitably prepared cow's horns were also employed for this purpose.

There is no biblical reference to children being suckled by animals.

### Weaning

Weaning practices were intimately bound up with teething, solid food being normally introduced when the milk teeth first appeared, while the last breast feed was given when the final milk teeth erupted, usually somewhere between two and three years of age.

An apocryphal notation indicated the completion of

weaning at three years (2 Macc. 7:27). Isaac was probably weaned at the end of his second year (Gen. 21:8), but Hosea's wife weaned her daughter unusually early (1:8). In Babylonia and contemporary Egypt weaning also took place at about three years. Hannah probably nursed her baby for about three years (1 Sam. 1:24). The completion of weaning was an occasion for celebration: "And the child grew, and was weaned: and Abraham made a great feast the same day that Isaac was weaned" (Gen. 21:8). Weaning marked the only clear period of transition before puberty, and indeed, when weaned, the child was considered sufficiently grown to begin learning something of husbandry (2 Kings 4:18). As a suckling, a child had the opportunity to play away from the mother (Isa. 11:8) and could say notable things (Ps. 8:2, Isa. 8:4). But at weaning he was mature enough to behave himself (Ps. 131:2), enter a holy place (1 Sam. 1:24) and receive instruction: "Whom shall he teach knowledge? and whom shall he make to understand doctrine? them that are weaned from the milk, and drawn from the breasts" (Isa. 28:9).

We can hardly judge the eating habits of older children as told in biblical narrative. Doubtless bread was an early addition to the diet of young Hebrew children, as was also wine, or more probably, beer (Lam. 2:11,12, 4:4). An analysis of ancient Egyptian beer showed that it had been brewed from fermented barley while Egyptian bread was baked from soured barley and wheat grains sweetened with honey and leavened with yeast.[4] Certainly bread was an earlier addition than meat. It is unlikely that any significant quantities of meat were given to children prior to the completion of weaning, meat being considered adult fare: "even as unto babes . . . I have fed you with milk, and not with meat: for hitherto ye were not able to bear it" (1 Cor. 3:1,2). "For every one that useth milk . . . is a babe . . . But strong meat belongeth to them that are of full age" (Heb. 5:13,14).

Mosaic Law laid down detailed instructions on eating habits, to be observed by children as well as adults. Most kinds of meat and fish were permitted; a good many fowl, and all fruits and vegetables could be eaten. Pork was forbidden, as were all insects bar locusts (Lev. 11). Strangely enough the Pentateuch does not mention the eating of eggs, presumably because fowl were not yet domesticated at that time. Eggs are noted in Luke 11:12, and birds' eggs in Deut. 22:6. The egg of Job 6:6 is a doubtful translation: it most probably refers to the slimy juice of a marsh mallow.[1]

The principal meals were at midday, and in the evening, when flesh was eaten. Manna was gathered in the early morning (Exod. 16:21) with a view to the midday meal. Fellahs in present-day Palestine go out to work early without eating but sometimes stop at about 9:00 A.M. for a frugal meal of bread. Exod. 16:12 refers to bread taken in the morning.

There is one passage in Isaiah (7:14,15) that has given rise to some misconceptions regarding the diet of the child Immanuel: "Curds (also translated as butter) and honey shall he eat . . ." It has been thought that this passage underlines the common ancient belief in purging the newborn. In fact it does not really have a pediatric meaning at all, only an agricultural one. It refers not to the diet of a particular child to be born in a messianic age; far from it— it refers to the imminent devastation of Israel prophesied (correctly) by Isaiah, and a return to pastoral conditions owing to the destruction of all cultivation in a once fertile land.

### Infant Care

We are probably safe in assuming that neonatal mortality was heavy. That people were not unaware of neonatal deaths is evidenced by the hope of Isaiah "There shall be no more thence an infant of days" (65:20). A death is mentioned at the age of one day: during the night a mother is stated to have "overlaid" her infant (1 Kings 3:19).

The procedure following a live birth seems reasonably clear. The umbilical cord was cut (Ezek. 16:4), the infant was then washed, oiled (16:9) and salted (16:4). Salting was thought to harden and toughen the skin. The nature of the material used is uncertain; some consider that it was the pleasant smelling powdered myrtle leaves (Neh. 8:15, Isa. 41:19, 55:13). Thereafter swaddling clothes were applied.

There is no record of when infants were first put to the breast, but perusal of 1 Kings 3:21 would indicate that lactation was established on the third day. This passage, famous as the celebrated "Judgement of Solomon," is of interest in that it does mention two or three points regarding neonatal practice:

"And it came to pass the third day after that I was delivered, that this woman was delivered also . . . And this woman's child died in the night; because she overlaid it. And she arose at midnight, and took my son from beside me . . . and laid her dead child in my bosom. And when I arose in the morning to give my child suck, behold, it was dead: but when I had considered it . . . it was not my son which I did bear" (1 Kings 3:18–21).

It is clear from this narrative that the place of the newborn was at the mother's side. Also, that this was known to be a hazardous procedure, and associated with occasional infant deaths. Further, true to the keen powers of observation possessed by mothers, the dead baby was recognized to have been substituted.

A few more observations may also be made. Neither of the babies featuring in this drama was premature. In this day and age the incidence of prematurity among babies born of prostitutes is high in comparison to that of married women; in Solomon's time the profession of harlotry was rather more respectable, and there was no particular reason for a high incidence of premature births. Moreover, the infants were so much alike that one mother (evidently, like the other, a harlot; neither had a husband) seriously thought that she could switch them round: it is unlikely that both were premature. A mature baby whose death during the first few days is clearly sudden and unexpected is likely to have perished not of "overlaying" but of a severe infection or else of a congenital abnormality of a vital structure.

The harlot's love for her baby highlights the filial affection to be noted in many parts of the scriptures. "Can a mother forget her sucking child, that she should not have compassion on the son of her womb?" (Isa. 49:15). The story of Hannah's love for her son Samuel (1 Sam. 2:1ff,19) is touching; so is the lament of Rachel (Jer. 31:15, Matt. 2:18) and of Rizpah for her dead sons (2 Sam. 21:10). How great must have been Abraham's anguish when commanded by God to sacrifice his son! Surely Abraham protested? The rabbis divined his pain so acutely that they gave Abraham an opportunity to reply to God. There is a rabbinic gloss to God's order in Gen. 22:2 "Take now thy son, thine only one, whom thou lovest, Isaac, and get thee into the land of Moriah; and offer him there for a burnt offering." Abraham is credited with interjecting as follows:

GOD: Take now thy son!

ABRAHAM: I have two sons (Isaac and Ishmael).

GOD: Thine only son!

ABRAHAM: Each of them is an only son to his mother.

GOD: Whom thou lovest!

ABRAHAM: Have I a wall in my heart?

GOD: Isaac!

In contrast, Ezek. 16:5 refers to the abandonment and

exposure of children: "No eye pitied thee . . . to have compassion upon thee; but thou wast cast out in the open field . . . in the day that thou wast born."

Moses, legendarily premature, did not sleep in his mother's bed. She hid him for three months (Exod. 2:2), presumably in some form of cot or cradle. His mother is known to have been capable of making infant cribs, for when she could no longer hide him, she made for him an "ark of bulrushes" (2:3). According to Hebrew tradition babies commonly slept in wooden rocking cots.

Some primitive peoples, especially certain African tribes, carry their young on the mother's back. The early Egyptians did likewise, carrying their infants by slinging them in a shawl wrapped round the mother or elder sister, sometimes in front and sometimes behind. Possibly the archaic Hebrews had a similar custom, although the Bible mentions only that infants could be carried in the bosom (Num. 11:12, Ruth 4:16) or "borne upon her sides, and dandled upon her knees" (Isa. 66:12).

## Naming

The procedure for naming newborns evolved through biblical times. In Hebrew custom the children were given names immediately after birth. Ruth's child was named at birth (4:17); so were the patriarchs, and indeed, all those whose births are reasonably well recorded in the Hebrew Bible. Commonly the names given had relevance to the gestation. Isaac was born when his mother was already post-menopausal. She feared that all who heard of her remarkable gestation would laugh at her (Gen. 21:6), hence her son was called Isaac, which means "one will laugh" or "one will mock."

Esau was so called because the word means—as indeed

he was—hairy. Reasons are also given for such names as Joseph, Benjamin and others. Many New Testament names are basically Hebrew (Jesus, John, Judas, Thomas, Simon). It is only in Paul's surroundings that Greek names appear.

The name Moses is intriguing, being derived from an Egyptian word *mose* or *mes* meaning "child of." This would explain pure Egyptian names like Ramose (son of the god Ra) or Thuthmose (son of Thoth). Originally Moses was but a suffix, qualifying a god in the form of a prefix. The biblical redactors extirpated this bit of heathen nomenclature.

Either parent could name the child, although it was usually the mother: "Hannah . . . bare a son and called his name Samuel" (1 Sam. 1:20). The English rendering of the naming procedures in 2 Sam. 12:24 and in Isa. 7:14 are by no means as straightforward as would appear, being fraught with etymological uncertainties. A mother's wish could be overruled. Although Rachel, in dying, called her son Ben-oni, his father called him Benjamin (Gen. 35:18). Attendants called Elisabeth's son Zacharias; the mother demurred, insisting on John, whereupon the attendants appealed to the father (Luke 1:62). Ruth's baby was named by attendants (Ruth 4:17). A feature of the naming procedure was the son's right to take his father's name, and even an ancestor's name, in order to describe his origin and family, while his own name distinguished him as an individual. King David was met by "a man of the family of the house of Saul, whose name was Shimei, the son of Gera" (2 Sam. 16:5).

In the event of a man dying childless, levirate marriage ensured the continuation of his name (Deut. 25:6).

By the time of the New Testament, naming is delayed until the ceremony of circumcision (Luke 1:59, 2:21).

### Circumcision

Even if it coincide with the Sabbath (John 7:22,23) "he that is eight days old shall be circumcised among you, every male throughout your generations" (Gen. 17:12, Lev. 12:3; see also Gen. 21:4, Luke 1:59, 2:21, Philem. 3:5). This is the covenant (*Brit*) of circumcision (*Milah*) made with Abraham "And I will establish my covenant between thee and me and thy seed after thee throughout their generations for an everlasting covenant, to be a God unto thee and to thy seed after thee" (Gen. 17:7).

Circumcision is not so much a surgical procedure as a religious operation. It is important to appreciate this point. Current apologetics on behalf of circumcision as being cleaner, healthier and associated with less cancer of the penis and of the cervix uteri in the wife, are irrelevant. The operation is a devotional one, and in biblical times assumed a form of vicarious sacrifice. Instead of human and animal sacrifice the foreskin was substituted: "when ye offer oblations unto me, I will turn my face from you: for your solemn feast days, your new moons, and your circumcisions of the flesh have I rejected" (1 Esd. 1:31). Tentative steps in this direction were already made by the Canaanites who noted that their god Baal could be propitiated by means of a substitute: a child's foreskin was offered, or else the priests slashed themselves until the altar was covered with blood (1 Kings 18:28).

The offering of blood as propitiation for the life of the child is recalled in Ezekiel 16:6 and, in fact, this verse is repeated in circumcision ceremonies to this day: "I said unto thee, In thy blood live. Yea, I said unto thee, in thy blood live."

Abraham (Gen. 17:24), Ishmael (17:25), Isaac (21:4),

Moses (Exod. 4:25), the family and nation under Joshua (5:3,7) and the people of Shechem (Gen. 34:24) were circumcised with blades of flint. In the last instance the wounds became infected on the third day (34:25). During the reign of King Saul, *c.* 1,000 B.C.E., iron was available but there was no smith in Israel (1 Sam. 13:19). Until well after the time of Saul blades of flint were used, and when these were supplanted with iron, stone continued to serve as a handle for the blade.

The Hebrews were very proud of their circumcised state and circumcision came to be equated with purity and goodness (Deut. 10:26, 30:6, Jer. 4:4). Conversely, they were contemptuous of the uncircumcised (Gen. 34:14, Exod. 6:30, Judg. 14:3, 1 Sam. 17:36, 31:4, 2 Sam. 1:20, 1 Chron. 10:4, Jer. 6:10, 9:26, Ezek. 44:7,9, Acts 7:51). In this regard it may be noted that among the Egyptians, civilized long before the Hebrews, the pharaohs and nobles were generally circumcised at puberty or adolescence, so that the Hebrews, who learned much from the Egyptians, might have derived their pride from pharaonic as well as Abrahamitic sources (Gen. 10:12, 13:1).

In later centuries, when the uncircumcised Greeks ruled over Palestine, some of the Jewish youths became ashamed of their circumcised state, especially during the (nude) Greek games. These youths attempted to lengthen whatever was left of their foreskins and were called epispadians (1 Macc. 1:15). But the mass of Jews remained fiercely proud of their denuded organs and forced circumcision on idolatrous or fearful Jews (1 Macc. 1:48,60,61, 2:46) and even on conquered tribes (Josephus, Antiquities, XIII, 9:1, 11:3).

Paul raised many arguments against circumcision (Rom. 2:25–29, 3:30, 4:9–12, 1 Cor. 7:18,19, Gal. 5:6, 6:15, Col. 2:11, 3:11) but, if we are to believe Luke (Acts 16:3), compromised in the case of Timothy, who had a Jewish mother.

Ritual circumcision may not be done earlier than eight days, happily precluding the possibility of hemorrhagic disease of the newborn. Since God's ordinances were given in order that one should live by them (Lev. 18:5) and not die by them, the operation may be postponed for reasons of health, and subsequent legislation forbade the operation in the presence of jaundice, familial bleeding disorders or, indeed, any sickness.

Little is known of the method of circumcision in ancient days. There are few documents available, though Josephus mentions briefly that "a surgeon" did the operation (Antiquities, XX, 2:4). It has been thought that the operation might have been no more than an amputation of the prepuce without reflecting the mucosa off the glans, this being the method among Moslems and Karaites. Exposure of the glans was possibly instituted at the time of the Maccabees, or as late as after the Bar Kochba rebellion (135 c.e.). At any rate the Mishnah (Sab. 12:2), completed in the second century of the Christian era, insists on reflecting the mucosa off the glans.

There is no biblical mention of female circumcision but there are legends that the Hebrews (Sarah, Hagar, Mary) practised it, as do Africans and Arabs to this day.

### Swaddling

In Babylonia, whence Hebrew culture was originally derived, swaddling of infants was apparently widely practised, and for a period of 40 days since it was believed that this procedure afforded some measure of protection against the evil demons of disease that plagued the Babylonian mind. Only after the completion of 40 days was it safe to take the infant out of swaddling clothes and out of the house, for by this time the infant was able to withstand the onslaughts of the demons lurking without. To this day Persian infants are swaddled and not taken out of the house or tent for 40 days.

But in Egypt, a country that also left a stamp on the culture of the Hebrews, swaddling was not practised. The newborns were wrapped in linen cloths and thereafter they were largely naked until about 5 years of age.

The role of swaddling in the prevention of rickets appears to be a deciding factor. In sunny Egypt, infants did not develop rickety deformities and so did not require to be swaddled.

The rest of the Fertile Crescent was also reasonably sunny, but presumably the culture in that region dictated that infants were to be sheltered within the house or tent for a number of months- -possibly to guard against the attacks of demons. As a consequence, rickets was inevitable. The resultant bony deformities being commonplace, attempts were made to prevent these by means of swaddling.

The extent of the practice of swaddling in Israel is uncertain. Both Babylonian and Egyptian procedures in newborn routine must have influenced the Israelite custom. It was probably a rather common, if not standard procedure, and as likely as not, was carried out for the ritually complete period of 40 days. The number 40 is rather unique in biblical usage for it indicates the completion of a long, definitive and purposeful period of time; and after the age of 40 days Hebrew infants were presumably permitted to be taken outside of their habitation, and free of their swaddling bands.

Ezekiel refers to swaddling (16:4), and so does Job (38:9), both using Hebrew words derived from the same root. The author of the Wisdom of Solomon (7:4) and also Luke (2:7,12) refer to swaddling in similar Greek terms. It is possible that Luke visited Jerusalem (though one cannot infer this from Acts 21:17) and that he observed swaddling of infants there. More likely he drew an inference from Roman practice.

Swaddling is also referred to in the book of Lamentations (2:22), but in this case the English rendering is misleading. The Hebrew term is *tippeakh* and this root is also used in Lam. 2:20, being translated as "children of a span long." Other renderings for *tippeakh* have favored "dandled" but in fact this verb means neither dandled nor swaddled, nor is it a measure of distance. In both 2:20 and 2:22 of Lamentations the verb denotes "to bring forth children which are healthy and well developed." [1]

The whole cavalcade of life, from conception to birth, to swaddling and feeding and death, is summarized in the poem of the Wisdom of Solomon (7:1–6) written some 50 years B.C.E.:

> I myself also am mortal, like to all,
> And am sprung from one born of the earth,
> The man first formed;
> And in the womb of a mother was I moulded into flesh
> In the time of ten months,
> Being compacted in blood of the seed of man
> And pleasure that came with sleep.
> And I also, when I was born, drew in the common air,
> And fell upon the kindred earth,
> Uttering like all, for my first voice, the self-same wail.
> In swaddling clothes was I nursed, and with watchful
>   cares;
> For no king had any other beginning,
> But all men have one entrance into life,
> And a like departure.

## *REFERENCES*

1. van Selms, A. Professor of Semitic Languages, University of Pretoria (1959) : Personal communication
2. Ginzberg, L. (1956): *Legends of the Bible.* Simon & Schuster, New York
3. Brim, C. J. (1943) : *Journal of Nervous and Mental Disease,* 97: 656
4. Swift, F. R. (1966): *Microchemical Journal,* 11:216

# DEATH

Judging from the numerous infant burials excavated in Palestine, infant mortality must have been heavy and there must have been comparatively few living to the ripe old age of "threescore years and ten" (Ps. 90:10) "and if by reason of strength they be fourscore years, yet is their strength labour and sorrow" (Ps. 90:10). War, hunger and pestilence despatched them.

"To every thing there is a season, and a time to every purpose under the heaven: A time to be born and a time to die" (Eccles. 3:1,2). Nor could this time be known or postponed (Eccles. 8:8). Death was the grim reaper, the "harvestman" (Jer. 9:22) who finally carried all to the grave, man's "long home" (Eccles. 12:5).

## Last Words

Jacob said his last words and blessings to his sons (Gen. 49:1–32) "and when Jacob had made an end of commanding his sons, he gathered up his feet into the bed, and yielded up the ghost" (Gen. 49:33).

Joseph's parting words were few (Gen. 50:24,25) and those of Moses many (Deut. 33:1–29). David ended his days with uncharitable instructions (1 Kings 2:1–9). Hezekiah's impassioned plea for life (2 Kings 20:3) occasioned God's "I will add unto thy days fifteen years" (2 Kings 20:6). Mattathias' last words were of patriotism (1 Macc. 2:49–69).

Jesus' last words on the cross include six different utterances, not all of which can be considered historical. "Father, forgive them, for they know not what they do" (Luke 23:34) is spurious; it is not found in the earliest manuscripts and it is not in keeping with one who fought the Romans and did not turn his other cheek to them (John 18:22,23). Perhaps most of the remaining utterances could be historical, that about being forsaken by God (Mark 15:34), about "I thirst" and "It is finished" (John 19:28,30) and about his spirit with God and his companions with him in paradise (Luke 23:43, 46).

### Suicide and Sacrifice

Suicide is rare in primitive societies. The Hebrew Bible, which legislates on every aspect of life and death, is silent on suicide: there are no laws on it, though Gen. 9:5 has been interpreted as a prohibition against suicide.

Abimelech (Judg. 9:54), Samson (Judg. 16:28–30), Saul (1 Sam. 31:4), Ahitophel (2 Sam. 17:23) and Zimri (1 Kings 16:18) committed suicide. The tale of Judas' suicide (Matt. 27:5) is dubious. More likely he was ripped open by a Roman sword (Acts 1:18) in the battle of Gethsemane.

"Passing through the fire to Moloch" (Lev. 18:21, 20:2–5, 1 Kings 11:7, 2 Kings 23:10, 2 Chron. 28:3, Jer. 32:25) has been thought to be a form of human sacrifice, though modern scholars now generally feel that it was rather a pagan rite to Moloch stopping short of ritual murder.

Mesha, king of Moab, did not stop short. When he saw that his forces prevailed not against Israel "Then he took his eldest son . . . and offered him for a burnt offering upon the wall" (2 Kings 3:27) at which the god Chemosh was suitably appeased.

Hiel the Bethelite rebuilt Jerusalem by sacrificing his first and last born sons and incorporating them into the walls and gates of the city (1 Kings 16:34).

The Hebrew rejection of human sacrifice is manifest in the story of the binding of Isaac (Gen. 22:1–13) and in the instructions to redeem the firstborn (Exod. 13:13,15, 34:20, Num. 18:15,16).

Cannibalism is noted in Deut. 28:53–57, 2 Kings 6:28, 29, Jer. 19:9, Lam. 4:10.

### Respect for the Dead

The Hebrew respect for the dead was manifest by a prompt and decent burial.

Prompt burial was desirable not only because a body decomposes rapidly in a hot climate but especially because it was considered humiliating and disrespectful to leave a corpse unburied, even the corpse of a criminal (Deut. 21:23).

It was also disrespectful to cremate a body in the manner of the Moabites who "burned the bones of the king of Edom into lime" (Amos 2:1). The Greeks burned their dead and placed the ashes in urns. The Romans also cremated their dead, leaving the ashes in repositories in tombs.

The men of Jabesh Gilead went to great risk in order to recapture the violated bodies of Saul and his sons which they then burned and buried (1 Sam. 31:12,13). The parallel and later account in 1 Chron. 10:12 omits the allusion to cremation. A second burial occurred later (2 Sam. 21:12–14).

Notwithstanding their abhorrence for cremation the Hebrews practised burning as a form of capital punishment for sexual immorality (Gen. 38:34, Lev. 20:14, 21:9). They also burned the bones of idolators but spared the bones of the faithful in their sepulchres (2 Kings 23:16–18).

Abraham made haste to bury Sarah (Gen. 23:1–19) and Rachel was buried at a roadside where she died (Gen. 35:19). Haste was imperative in clearing the land of the defilement of death (Ezek. 39:11–14) lest there be carcasses under the feet (Isa. 14:18–20), unburied, to be devoured by beast and bird (1 Sam. 17:44,46, 2 Sam. 21:10, 1 Kings 13:24–28, 14:11, 2 Kings 9:10, Ps. 79:3, Jer. 6:4, Ezek. 29:5).

When Hezekiah was buried "all Judah and the inhabitants of Jerusalem did him honour at his death" (2 Chron. 32:33). Ben Sira (38:16) urged an honorable burial, and Tobit rescued a Jewish corpse (2:3,4) and buried it at the peril of his own life (2:7,8).

Jewish respect for the dead is so marked that it is hard to credit Christ with the brutal dismissal "Let the dead bury their dead" (Matt. 8:22, Luke 9:60). This is not a Jewish attitude and is probably contributed by one whose words and personality came to be absorbed within the figure called Christ: the censorious John the Baptist, who considered the mass of Jews to be spiritually dead.

How different was the attitude of a pagan pharaoh who, when approached by Joseph for permission to bury Jacob, replied "Go up, and bury thy father" (Gen. 50:6).

Curiously, the Christian attitude to the dead has been in reverse direction to that of Christ. They have gone to the other extreme: excessive reverence. A pathological reverence for the dead resulted in churches being filled with the bones and relics of saints, so much so that they became veritable anatomical museums and the early pagans called them charnel houses. To this day the Catholic church traffics in the bones of saints.

Jewish religious development was more sane and never permitted the honored dead to usurp the place of the living.

The sabbath may be profaned in order to save the life of a day-old baby but not in order to bury king David (Talmud, Shabbat 151b). If a marriage procession and a funeral cortège meet at an intersection the marriage procession takes precedence (Ketubot 17a).

## Burial Rites

In early times the eyes of the corpse were closed (Gen. 46:4) with a kiss (Gen. 50:1) and it was dressed in representative garments, such as the cloak of the prophet (1 Sam. 28:14) or the sword of the warrior (Ezek. 32:27). The body was laid in its grave stretched out straight or lying on the left side with the knees drawn up toward the chin. Aromatic spices might be burned near the body (2 Chron. 16:14, 21:19, Jer. 34:5). Since dust was to return to dust (Gen. 3:19) there had to be intimate contact between earth and corpse. The mention of a coffin (Gen. 50:26) for Joseph is quite exceptional and reflects the Egyptian culture of that period.

In later biblical times, as reflected in the Jewish customs described in the New Testament, some development had taken place in burial rites. After death the corpse was washed, this being based on rabbinical interpretation of Eccles. 5:15 "As he came forth of his mother's womb, naked shall he return to go as he came." Since he arrived in liquid, he must be washed in parting (Acts 9:37). The body might also be scented with aromatic spices (John 12:3,7, 19:39,40, Mark 16:1, Luke 24:1) and wrapped in linen (John 19:40, Mark 15:46, Matt. 27:59, Luke 23:53, Acts 5:6) to secure body and limbs (John 11:44) while a separate cloth covered the head (John 11:44, 20:7). The corpse was placed in an open bier (2 Sam. 3:31) within the house (Acts 9:37) before removal to the burial place.

### Embalming

Embalming is un-Jewish but was perhaps practised more often than the records reveal. In an Egyptian culture it is understandable that "Joseph commanded his servants the physicians to embalm his father: and the physicians embalmed Israel" (Gen. 50:2). Joseph was also embalmed (Gen. 50:26). Aristobulus II (67–63 B.C.E.), Hasmonean ruler of Judea, was poisoned and "His dead body also lay, for a good while, embalmed in honey, till Antony afterwards sent it to Judea, and caused him to be buried in the royal sepulchre" (Josephus, Antiquities, XIV, 7:4).

Embalming required some 70 days to complete and the technique reached its acme in Egypt during the 18th dynasty (1550–1350 B.C.E.). According to Herodotus, who visited Egypt about 450 B.C.E., the brain was first removed via the nose (an improbable achievement!). Thereafter the viscera were removed from abdomen and thorax (the heart was left *in situ*) and placed in jars. The body, now little more than bone, cartilage, muscle and skin, was then dehydrated by means of the liberal application of various salts and solutions thought to be mostly sodium carbonate. Then the cranium and nasal cavities plus the chest and abdomen were stuffed with linen impregnated with resinous pastes and spices and finally the mummy was elaborately wrapped with enormous lengths of linen.

### Burial Places

The hope of the dying Hebrew was that he should be "gathered unto his fathers." This was not necessarily a literal placement, as in the instances of Abraham (Gen. 25:8),

147

Moses (Deut. 31:16), Joshua and his generation (Judg. 2:9, 10), David (1 Kings 2:10, 11:21) and Lazarus (Luke 16:22). However, in many instances there were family graves and tombs, and Isaac (Gen. 35:29), Jacob (Gen. 49:29,30), Gideon (Judg. 8:32), Samson (Judg. 16:31), Asahel (2 Sam. 2:32), Barzilai (2 Sam. 19:37), Jehoshaphat (2 Chron. 21:1) and Mattathias (1 Macc. 2:69) were literally gathered unto their fathers. Hezekiah was buried in the sepulchre of a more remote ancestor, David (2 Chron. 32:33). Nehemiah expressed a wish to be buried in the city of his father's sepulchres (2:5) and Ruth the Moabite elected to die not with her own people, but among the graves of her Hebrew mother-in-law (1:17). The proselyte king Izates, and his mother Helena, of Adiabene, were buried in tombs near Jerusalem (Josephus, Antiquities, XX, 4:3). The wicked Jehoram was buried "in the city of David, but not in the sepulchre of the kings" (2 Chron. 21:20).

Tombs were of varying origin and architecture. The simplest were no more than a grave marked by a pillar. Absalom had prepared one such for himself (2 Sam. 18:18) though in fact he met an unexpected end and was buried in a pit and covered with stones (2 Sam. 18:17). Jacob erected a pillar over Rachel's grave (Gen. 35:20).

Caves were popular, the most famous being the cave of Machpelah in which were buried Sarah (Gen. 23:19), Abraham, Isaac and Jacob. A similar cave was alleged to have held the body of Jesus (John 19:41,42, 20:1, Mark 15:46) though it is more likely that, as a convicted felon, the Romans would have thrown his body into a common grave. There were cemeteries for those who owned no land for a family tomb or for malefactors and strangers (2 Kings 23:6, Isa. 53:9, Jer. 26:23, Matt. 27:7). A cave was also used as a tomb for Lazarus of Bethany (John 11:38) and for Elisha (2 Kings 14:21) whose dead bones miraculously resurrected a corpse.

The more elaborate tombs were whitewashed (Matt. 23:27) and some were veritable mausoleums (1 Macc. 13:27–29, Josephus Antiquities XIII, 6:6). Unlike the Egyptian palaces of death or the sepulchres of the Canaanites (2 Kings 23:16) the Hebrew burials were devoid of feeding vessels, jewelry and assorted funeral furniture. Aside from spices, excavations have revealed that oil lamps were the most characteristic funeral furniture among the Hebrews. However, when the sepulchre of David and Solomon was plundered by Hyrcanus and shortly thereafter by Herod, in the first century B.C.E., silver coins and golden furniture were found (Antiquities, XVI, 7:1).

If the poor, the foreigner and the criminal were interred in a common cemetery, individual graves might be situated anywhere. Samuel (1 Sam. 25:1), Joab (1 Kings 2:34), Manasseh (2 Kings 21:18) and Amon (2 Kings 21:26) were buried near their homes, the expected place for the graves of kings (Isa. 14:18). Deborah, Rebekah's nurse, was buried under an oak (Gen. 35:8), Rachel was buried at a roadside near Bethlehem (Gen. 35:19) and Saul under an oak tree (1 Chron. 10:12).

The most famous grave of all is that of Moses, whom God himself buried "in a valley in the land of Moab, over against Beth-peor: but no man knoweth of his sepulchre unto this day" (Deut. 34:6). Mrs. C. F. Alexander has caught the spirit of lonely grandeur in two stanzas of her poem, "The Burial of Moses":

By Nebo's lonely mountain,
On this side Jordan's wave,
In a vale of the land of Moab
There lies a lonely grave;
And no man knows that sepulchre,
And no man saw it e'er

For the Angels of God upturned the sod,
And laid the dead man there.

Perchance the bald old eagle
On grey Beth-peor's height,
Out of his rocky eyrie
Looked on the wondrous sight.
Perchance the lion stalking
Still shuns that hallowed spot,
For beast and bird have seen and heard
That which man knoweth not.

## Mourning

Subdued mourning and gentlemanly decorum were far removed from Semitic custom. A healthy oriental emotionalism characterized the lamentations for the dead. Loud mourning was good and proper (Jer. 34:5, Ezek. 27:30–32, Joel 1:8, Sira 38:16–18, Mark 5:38, Matt. 9:23, Acts 9:39) and professional lamenters were employed (Jer. 9:17,18,20).

Rachel, the "tribal mother" was pictured as mourning her children (Jer. 31:15) on their way to exile in Babylon (Jer. 14:2, 22:10, 31:16,17). Abraham mourned for Sarah (Gen. 23:2), Jacob for Joseph (Gen. 37:34) and David for Saul and Jonathan (2 Sam. 1:12). David's eulogies are tragic and moving. His elegy over Saul and Jonathan (2 Sam. 1:19–27) is poetry at its most magnificent. He also weeps for Abner (2 Sam. 3:32–34) and has a heartbroken cry for his wayward son "O my son Absalom, my son, my son Absalom! would God I had died for thee, O Absalom, my son, my son!" (2 Sam. 18:33, 19:1–4). How honest and genuine is this response of a bereaved father and how genuine and touching the grief of Rizpah for her sons (2 Sam. 21:10). The mood of Jacob, thinking his son Joseph to be dead, is also accurately captured in all the pathos of a stricken father "And all his sons and all his daughters rose up to comfort him; but he refused to be comforted; and he said, For I will go down into the grave unto my son mourning" (Gen. 37:35). The very silence of Job's comforters spoke volumes (2:13).

Mourners did more than place a black armband on their jackets. They rent their clothes (Gen. 37:34, Lev. 10:6, 2 Sam. 1:11, 3:31, 13:31, 15:32, Esther 4:1, Job 1:20, 2:12), donned sackcloth and put ashes on their heads (Gen. 37:34, 38:14, 2 Sam. 3:31, 14:2, 15:32, 21:10, 1 Kings 21:27, Esther 4:1, Job 2:12, Ps. 35:13, Isa. 20:2, 22:12, Jer. 6:26, 48:37, Ezek. 27:30,31, Dan. 9:3, Joel 1:8,13, Matt. 11:21, Luke 10:13). They sat or lay on the dust of the earth (2 Sam. 13:31, Job 2:13, Mic. 1:10), barefoot (2 Sam. 15:30, Ezek. 24:17,23), spurning ornaments (Exod. 33:4), oil (2 Sam. 14:2, Dan. 10:3) and "neither dressed his feet, nor trimmed his beard, nor washed his clothes" (2 Sam. 19:24). Commonly the beard was shaved off (Isa. 15:2, Jer. 41:5, 48:37), the head shaved (Job 1:20, Isa. 15:2, 22:12, Jer. 16:6, 48:37, Ezek. 27:31, Amos 8:10, Mic. 1:16) and the headdress removed (Lev. 10:6, Ezek. 24:17,23) though a grieving David and his company covered their heads (2 Sam. 15:30).

It was also a custom in Canaan for mourners to cut their flesh in their grief. This self-mortification was forbidden to the Hebrews (Lev. 19:28, Deut. 14:1, Jer. 16:6, 41:5).

Since the presence of death defiled a house, it was forbidden to eat of the food therein (Num. 19:14, Hos. 9:4) and neighbors had to provide (2 Sam. 3:35, Jer. 16:7, Ezek. 24:17). Hallowed food (Deut. 26:13,14), good food, meat and wine were avoided (Dan. 10:3) though wine might have been used to cheer the excessively sad (Prov. 31:6,7).

Mourners also observed a varying period of fasting (1 Sam. 31:13, 2 Sam. 1:12, 3:35, 1 Kings 21:27, Dan. 9:3, Joel 1:14, Zech. 7:5, Judith 8:6). David exemplified the behavior of some parents who empty themselves with prayer and weeping and have no more tears to shed when their child dies (2 Sam. 12:15–23). "And he said, While the child was yet alive, I fasted and wept: for I said, Who can tell whether God will be gracious to me, that the child may live? But now he is dead, wherefore should I fast? Can I bring him back again? I shall go to him, but he shall not return to me. And David comforted Bathsheba his wife . . ." (2 Sam. 12:22–24).

Mourning for the dead lasted 7 days (Sira 22:12) after which there was a ceremony of purification (Num. 31:19). Jacob was mourned 70 days by the Egyptians (Gen. 50:3) and a further 7 days by his son Joseph (Gen. 50:10). Saul was mourned for 7 days (1 Sam. 31:13) and the Talmud (Sanhedrin 108b) interprets the 7-day delay in the flood (Gen. 7:10) as a mark of respect to Methuselah.

Moses (Deut. 34:8) and Aaron (Num. 20:29) were mourned for 30 days and there was an annual lament for Jephtha's daughter (Judg. 11:40).

Several of the ancient mourning customs are still observed by orthodox Jews, in particular 7 days of intense mourning (*shiva*), followed by a period of lesser mourning up to the 30th day (*shloshim*), and a yearly recollection (*yahrzeit*).

### REFERENCE

Rabinowicz, H. (1964): *A Guide To Life: Jewish Laws and Customs of Mourning.* Jewish Chronicle Publications, London

# THE ANATOMY OF THE SOUL:

## Dilemmas and Difficulties in the Soular System

Dreams. Perhaps it is a vision of the departed that sparks the belief that he has never died. Somewhere a memory lingers, someplace a remnant remains.

Among the Bantu the ghosts of the dead—especially kings—are virtually deified, but the souls do not wander away; they remain members of the clan and after some years may even be reincarnated into a newborn who is then given the same name as the departed.

In New Guinea the Papuan souls go to the spirit world at the summit of one of the high mountains.

The souls of the Aztecs went to a dreary underworld. Those dead of drowning, lightning, leprosy and dropsy lifted their souls to the more attractive heavenly abode of the rain-god, while the finest heaven, that of the sun-god, was reserved for warriors killed in battle and women dead in childbirth. Warrior souls accompanied the sun to its zenith in the guise of humming birds, while obstetric souls were moths escorting the sun to the horizon.

Among the Apache Indians a portion of the soul of a newborn child remains within the cord and placenta. This is not buried for fear that a stray dog will dig it up and consume it, thus injuring the child. Instead it is tied in a bundle of cloth and placed in a fruit-bearing tree which is yearly renewed by growth.

Not only the American Indians have happy hunting grounds. The souls of departed Japanese children frolic in a heavenly garden of bright flowers and gay butterflies.

In Bali an essence of soul inheres in locks of hair, nail cuttings, saliva, or even in a physical likeness in a doll. A portion of the soul is captured within them, and if they are ritually harmed the individual will suffer. Even a person's shadow has enough soul to lend itself to machinations by evil witches, views which were also not unknown in early Greece and Egypt.

In hieroglyphic the Egyptian soul is represented as a basket of fire, a heron, a ram or a hawk with a human face. If not all Egyptians, then at least the nobility possessed a *ka,* a soul. After death the *ka* was weighed against a feather, and if found wanting, was devoured by wild animals, but if it pleased the gods, the soul continued a sybaritic existence.

The Egyptians also pictured a portion of the soul within the placenta and this was preserved in a "bundle of life," a revered object. The royal placenta was carried as a symbol before the pharaoh, especially on ceremonial occasions, and this practice was continued up to the time of the Ptolemies (about 300 B.C.E.). The placenta was opened and scattered at the conclusion of the reign. During the 4th, 5th and 6th dynasties there existed an official known as the "Opener of the King's placenta." [1,2]

Moslems say that the souls of the faithful assume the form of snow-white birds which nestle under the throne of Allah until the resurrection. Sufis (Moslem mystics) hold that the soul yearns for reunion with its Creator, and this union could be achieved in gradual stages of mystical experience culminating in the final ecstasy of union.

The Babylonians did not believe that death brought obliteration. There was a dreary survival in a wretched realm of the infernal god Nergal. The goddess Ishtar spent a period in hell.

The Persian Zoroaster preached a heaven of light and a hell of darkness.

The Chinese revere their ancestors without having developed any real concept of soul. They never recognized individual immortality. Survival was conceived in terms of everlasting influence in society, the immortality of worth, work and words.

Hindus (and western gnostic sects such as the theosophists) have well developed concepts of soul whose object is not everlasting life but everlasting extinction and absorption into the All-Soul. Various denominations limited the extent of absorption.

### The Hebrew Soul

Despite their Egyptian contacts, or perhaps because of them, the Hebrews rejected the grossness of Egyptian concepts of soul and contained the soul within the body, both perishing together. But they did retain Egyptian views on the placental soul. Thus said Abigail to the fugitive David: "Yet a man is risen to pursue thee, and to seek thy soul: but the soul of my lord shall be bound in the bundle of life with the Lord thy God: and the souls of thine enemies, them shall he sling out, as out of the middle of a sling" (1 Sam. 25:29).

The Hebrew biblical view of the body-soul relationship is strictly monistic: neither could exist without the other. In any event, the very concept of soul is hazy and the meaning

*155*

of the term is probably closer to personality than to soul.

Whatever this unique substance, it resided in the blood, both in man and in animals: "For the soul (Hebrew, *nefesh*) is in the blood." (Gen. 9:4, Lev. 17:11,14, Deut. 12:23) and blood might not be eaten (Gen. 9:4, Lev. 3:17, 7:26,27, 17:10,12,14, 19:26, Deut. 12:16,23,24,25, 15:23, 1 Sam. 14:32–34).

During the 8th century c.e., Anan ben David, founder of the schismatic sect known as the Karaites, held that Lev. 17:11 meant that the blood itself was the soul, the life, but less literal interpreters from the orthodox ranks disputed this identity, maintaining that the soul, the vitalism (oxygen ?) was in the blood but not identical with it.

The early Hebrews had no real concept of an afterlife. While Job (4th century b.c.e.?), unlike some of David's contemporaries (Ps. 14:1, 53:1), accepted God, he rejected immortality: "If a man die, shall he live again?" (Job 14:14). David also rejected immortality: "As for man, his days are as grass: as a flower of the field, so he flourisheth. For the wind passeth over it, and it is gone; and the place thereof shall know it no more" (Ps. 103:15,16). Man would like to live forever, to immortalize his land in his name (Ps. 49:11), but he perishes like the beasts and is laid in the grave like sheep and death feeds on him (Ps. 49:12,14, Eccles. 3:19).

The end of man was dust "for dust thou art, and unto dust shalt thou return" (Gen. 3:19). For the biblical Hebrews a man lived on, physically and spiritually, only in his children, and with such a philosophy he was perfectly content. Adam achieved immortality through procreation.

For the early Hebrews the reward of a good life was a long life ("that thou mayest prolong thy days" Exod. 20:12, Deut. 4:40, 5:33, 11:9, 22:7, 32:47) with a happy progeny. The soul featured little in the biblical scheme, but round about 300–400 b.c.e., and for reasons which are not at all clear—perhaps contact with Zoroastrian thought on soul and resurrection was one factor—the soul was accorded a more permanent existence.

In the earliest books of the Hebrew Bible there are a few exceedingly vague allusions (Num. 16:30, 1 Sam. 28:13–19, Ps. 49:15, Isa. 26:19, 38:17,18, Job 17:16) to an underworld or afterlife, but in the later canon there are more definite affirmations. About 300 B.C.E. the author of Ecclesiastes wrote "Then shall the dust return to the earth as it was: and the spirit shall return unto God who gave it" (12:7). The Book of Daniel, also penned rather late (170 B.C.E. ?) notes "And many of them that sleep in the dust of the earth shall awake, some to everlasting life, and some to shame and everlasting contempt" (12:2).

Ezekiel's vision (Chapter 37) of the resurrected dry bones helped to foster belief in physical resurrection, and later Talmudic speculations (Gen. Rabbah 28:3, Lev. Rabbah 18) suggested that the most indestructible bone, the sacred bone, called *luz*, the *os sacrum*, would act as the pivot about which the rest of the body would be built up.

The Talmud, a kind of collection of minutes of rabbinical meetings over 1,000 years, was completed in the 5th century C.E. Though it granted the soul a separate identity, the Talmud did not depart from the earlier monistic cohesion of body and soul. Their relationship was likened to a sword within a scabbard. At no time did Talmudic views approach the dualistic concepts of Hellenism whereby a good soul inhabited an inherently evil body. For the Hebrew the two were a unity, and for this reason the Talmud could not countenance any mortification of the flesh, as being equally damaging to the soul. Asceticism, celibacy, self-inflicted injury and suicide are foreign to Jewish thought. Even the Nazarite, who denied his body the occasional pleasures of wine, was considered a sinner.

The soul was thought to have been created, kept for future use in *guf*, a celestial store-house for souls contained within *Araboth*, the 7th heaven. A pretty tale relates that at conception the Lord commanded a reluctant soul to be taken up by Lailah, the Angel of the Night, and deposited within the fertile womb. At death the soul returned to God. Metempsychosis, the transmigration of souls within many bodies, was unknown to the Talmud, though it was taught by a much later (15th and 16th centuries) esoteric sect known as the Cabbalists.

Later Hebrews did not all take kindly to this new emphasis on the importance and immortality of the soul. At the time of Jesus most Jews accepted the belief, but the Sadducee sect rejected it as a theological novelty not in keeping with the ancient traditions. They also rejected demonology, messianic beliefs and resurrection (Luke 20:27) as contrary to the teachings of Moses.

Subsequent rabbinic generations strengthened the belief in an immortal soul, while the 12th century physician-rabbi Maimonides even declared in favor of physical resurrection, a concept which though mouthed on ceremonial occasions, has nevertheless been tacitly dropped.

This presented no difficulty, for Judaism has no dogmas; it is a religion without a theology, and in any event the soul was never important in Jewish history. Though the Talmud accorded it a respectable status, it could not compete with the soul-less teachings of the Hebrew Bible. The Talmudic tales were never dogmas, and were always characterized by charity and tolerance. The Talmudic writings were semi-humorous and lacked the deadly earnestness of Christian teachings. Discussions on the Hebrew soul were marked by the amused detachment appropriate to a sport. The soul was never more than a half-serious game, a subject for entertaining casuistry.

Though Hebrew prayers do refer to the immortal soul —infrequently at that—contrary prayers are also known: "It is not the dead who will praise you . . . it is we" (the living) "who will bless you from now to eternity" (from Ps. 115:17–18). Significantly, the *Kaddish,* the Hebrew (actually Aramaic) prayer for the dead, recited by mourners at the graveside and annually thereafter, mentions nothing about the departed, nothing about the soul, about eternal life; indeed not even a single word about death. The *Kaddish* is simply a paean of praise to God.

The this-worldly accent of Judaism resulted in Hebrew cultures which frowned on all mysticism (Lev. 19:26,31, 20:6,27, Deut. 18:10,11, 1 Sam. 28:7ff, 1 Chron. 10:13, Isa. 8:19, 47:13). Aside from occasional small sects, the great mass of Jews throughout the centuries took no interest in matters like occultism, spiritualism, witchcraft, and the various healing cults, shrines and waters.

Chief Rabbi I. Jakobovits, PhD, of Britain, penned a 350-page book [3] on Jewish medical ethics containing virtually no discussion on the Jewish soul. The nine pages on abortion are introduced by the statement that in Jewish Law abortion is unrelated to theological considerations.

The late chief rabbi of England edited an inspiring anthology[4] of some 400 commentaries on Jewish historical, cultural and spiritual values. Only three of these allude to the soul, and then not in serious vein, but in amusing Talmudic *haggadah* (fable).

A similar American volume[5] on Jewish deed, doctrine and destiny features more than 500 sections with virtually nothing on the Jewish soul.

Rabbi L. I. Rabinowitz, lately chief rabbi in Johannesburg, left three volumes[6] of sermons, 215 in all, only one of which deals with the afterlife, and then in a reticent and cursory fashion recalling the attitude of the Preacher who, though he had no illusions about the fate of man, qualified his view with a vague doubt: "For that which befalleth the sons of men befalleth beasts; even one thing befalleth them: as the one dieth, so dieth the other; yea, they have all one breath; so that a man hath no pre-eminence over a beast . . . all go unto one place; all are of the dust, and all turn to dust again" (Eccles. 3:19–20), and his concluding doubt follows in the next verse: "Who knoweth the spirit of man that goeth upward, and the spirit of the beast that goeth downward to the earth" (3:21).

## The Christian Soul

"What shall it profit a man if he gain the whole world and lose his own soul?" (Matt. 16:26). With the advent of Christ and especially of Paul, the breach with Judaism was fundamental and complete.

As an eschatological faith, a religion of preparation for death, for eternal life or eternal perdition, Christianity was at once plunged into the gloomy business of grooming the soul for its future. Instead of Judaism's accent on earthly life, Christianity's teaching accents everlasting life and resurrection (Matt. 17:2–10, 25:46, 28:1–7, Luke 18:30, John 3:15–18, 5:21,24, 6:40,54, Rom. 2:7, 1 Cor. 15:53,54, 1 Tim. 6:16, 2 Tim. 1:10). Instead of Judaism's vague mention of an even vaguer *Sheol* (Underworld), the gospels, unlike the Hebrew Bible, suffer from the handicap of being a product of a messianic culture, and as a consequence present a very real, fully developed and well-peopled Hades of everlasting punishment, damnation, outer darkness, lakes of fire and hell fire (Matt. 3:12, 5:22,29ff, 8:12, 10:15,28, 11:20ff, 12:40, 13:40ff,50, 16:18, 18:8,9, 22:13, 23:33, 25:30,41,46, Mark 3:29, 6:11, 9:43–48, Luke 3:17, 12:5, 16:19–31!, 2 Thess.

1:8,9, James 3:6, 1 Pet. 3:18–20, 2 Pet. 2:4, Rev. 2:10, 14:10, 11, 19:20, 20:10,14,15, 21:8).

Under the influence of Darwin, that great Higher Critic Julius Wellhausen postulated that religions also evolve, ever better, ever more moral. But religion is not biology. It does not evolve ever better. Instead, periodically, it throws up religious or moral geniuses. At other times it is plunged into messianic and ethical gloom, and Christianity arose from just such a religious culture.

The Christians introduced a dichotomy of body and soul, the latter being active, free, pure, good and incorruptible, the body incurably evil, a source of sin and passion. The perishable body was incompatible with immortality (1 Cor. 15:50). This philosophy permitted, nay encouraged, celibacy, mortification of the flesh, and the infliction of the most hideous tortures on the body in order to save the soul.

Yet Christianity was not the first to separate body and soul. The Greeks had done so, and Plato in particular held that the soul was immortal, housed for a short period in a body which he likened to a prison. Platonic doctrines had a marked influence in shaping the soul of the Christians. The Greeks, and the Greek-influenced Romans, had ruled Jewish Palestine for 300 years before Christ. Contrariwise, Greek philosophy prepared the western world for acceptance of the Christian soul.

Like Plato, Augustine (4th–5th century) emphasized the immateriality of the soul. The doctrines of the Manichaeans, a sect to which he originally belonged, associated matter with evil, and were not without influence on Christianity. In later centuries Christian philosophers (in particular Descartes, 17th century) repeated the views of Plato that the soul was a distinct entity separable from the body. Thomas Aquinas (13th century) sought to show that the existence of an immortal soul could be proved by the unaided reason.

Aristotle saw differently. In the last analysis he was a biologist, adopting a monistic philosophy of unity of body and soul. And not only man was accorded a soul, but all animal and all plant life as well had a spiritual essence integrally associated with it. Aristotle saw no fundamental distinction between soul and mind.

Both Plato and Aristotle agreed, however, on another aspect of immortality. They recognized that men seek immortality in their descendants and their creative works, and in fact, in this respect, both philosophers are to be counted among the immortals.

For close on 2,000 years Christian theologians and philosophers have debated the soul, personal salvation, everlasting life and eternal perdition. There is an especially large body of writing concerning the time of entry of the soul into the body. Like the Stoics, Augustine denied that the soul entered at conception, but Tertullian (3rd century) agreed with Pythagoras that the soul entered at the instant of conception, a view held by modern Christians and modern Hindus who, consistently enough, reckon their age from conception rather than from birth. Modern Moslem teaching is that the soul enters the embryo at the age of 120 days.

Christian debates on the soul were hardly amicable games. If the truth be told, clerical pronouncements unleashed acrimonious and intolerant furies leading all too often to hurried and heated liberation of thousands of souls from their mortal remains.

But Darwin taxed the dialectic of the theologians, and in the past 100 years, liberal Christianity, intent on establishing a Christian ethic, has generally tended to gloss over the problems of eschatology, and has either symbolized the horrific pictures of hell or else, like the "de-mythologiser"

Bultmann, simply ignored these awkward portions of the gospels as though these teachings of Christ didn't exist, and has increasingly defined hell as the "soul's alienation from God" while heaven is proximity to or absorption into God.

These vague platitudes come dangerously close to Hindu-Buddhist doctrines in which Nirvana is absorption of the soul into Brahman, the All-Soul, and hell is consignment by virtue of prior *karma* (merit) to rebirth on earth, and not only within the bodies of humans, but, and this seems eminently reasonable, within animal bodies as well.

But perhaps the Christian All-Soul, God, is not to be equated with the Hindu All-Soul, the former All-Embracing, Living, All-Feeling, the latter All-Embracing, Existing, All-Unfeeling. Yet the discerning thinker will notice how the passage of time has brought two irreconcilable All-Souls almost non-face to non-face. Perhaps in another 1,000 years, as the God of Abraham, Moses, Jesus and Mahomet recedes more and more into the background to assume the role of a Deity Emeritus, perhaps then the fusion will be complete.

## Dissectors of the Soul

Hippocratic writers considered the brain as the seat of the soul. Herophilus of Alexandria (3rd century B.C.E.) favored the ventricular cavities as harboring the soul. Galen (2nd century C.E.) said the soul was in the substance of the brain and not in the ventricles, for the very good reason that penetrating injuries of the ventricles may deprive the individual of sensory and motor activities but they are not necessarily immediately fatal as would be expected if the soul resided in the ventricular system.[7]

The soul must have had extensions to the rest of the body for Greeks and Romans held that it departed through the death wound and momentarily during a sneeze.

Little more of any consequence was heard of the location of the soul during the Middle Ages except that excreta and hair and nail clippings were also credited with the essence of soul.

Prominent Arabic and Jewish physicians like Avicenna and Maimonides (both 12th century) did not question the soul, though Maimonides made the intriguing suggestion that perhaps only those who merited an immortal soul, especially the learned, had one.

In the 15th century the Papal Inquisitors considered the possibility of the soul temporarily leaving the body, especially in witches. James Sprenger, co-author of the "Malleus Maleficarum," the textbook of the Inquisition, dealing with the detection, interrogation, torture and disposal of witches and sundry heretics, doubted that witches attend their Sabbats by means of wandering souls issuing from their mouths, yet he gave serious consideration to this view: "They lie down to sleep on their left side and then a sort of bluish vapour comes from their mouth, through which they can see clearly what is happening."

Nicholas Stensen of Denmark was a convert to Catholicism and a missionary in northern Europe. He is best known for his description of Stensen's duct but he also wrote a "Dissertation on the Anatomy of the Brain" in 1665, in which he claimed "It is very certain that it is the principal organ of the soul."

In the 17th century Descartes emphasized the Platonic views on the dichotomy of body and soul, and the Cartesian System also included the opinion that the soul resided in the pineal gland.

It was also known at that time that the body became lighter at death, from which the inference was drawn that the soul had departed.

In the middle 1700's an Italian priest, Francesco Emanuel Cangiamila, paid particular attention to the problem of the entry of the soul into the embryo. His "Embryologia Sacra" was a bestseller. His anxiety to baptize the fetus so that its unsaved soul might not perish with the mother, led him to urge frequent Caesarian section on the living and the dead.

Emanuel Swedenborg (late 18th century; born in Sweden, died penniless in Britain) spent half his adult life as a physiologist, mathematician, astronomer, metallurgist, inventor, geologist, paleontologist and economist, making creditable contributions in all these fields. He was especially interested in the anatomy of the brain, and wrote original and searching opinions on cerebral tracts and functions. When, at the age of 56 years he "got religion" (he conversed with angels, wrote a book, "Divine Love," founded a Church, still extant) and abandoned science for mysticism, he sought to locate the soul on the basis of his anatomical studies.

Thomas Samuel von Soemerring numbered the cranial nerves, his system still being the one in use today. He was excited about the cerebral ventricles, evidently feeling that these cavities contained something more than material body, and in 1796 he titled his book *"On the Organ of the Soul."* Fortunately he first showed it to his friend Goethe, who advised that he change the title to *"On the Cerebral Endings of the Nerves"* and leave the soul to look after itself.[8]

The soul is not to be found in the Index of "Gray's Anatomy."

### Biological Problems in the Soular System

Whatever the desires of theology, whatever the trivia of spiritism, biological considerations place enormous hurdles in the way of a separate existence for the soul.

If the body has a soul the crucial question to be faced is "What portion of the body does it animate?"

There are staggering difficulties to associating the soul with any organ other than the brain. Nor will it help to say that the rest of the body also has a "spark" or "essence" of soul, for where "soul" is indefinable, undemonstrable and unverifiable, "spark" and "essence" have no meaning.

To grant something of a soul to trunk and limbs at once raises queries on the fate of this spiritual essence in the event of additions to, or subtractions from the body. Theologians commonly know little of surgery and nothing of teratology and their learned expositions have never considered how the soular status might be affected by amputations and excisions and by loss from the body of blood, semen, saliva, mucus, excreta, teeth, hair and nail clippings.

Conversely, there must be considered the role of added material, both human (blood, sperm, skin, kidney, and especially heart), animal (bone) and inert substances.

What of the addition of a pregnancy (soular symbiosis?) or of the tissues of a dead twin, a dermoid, a chimera? How many souls are involved in a monster with one brain and two bodies or two heads and one body? If the soul enters at conception and the embryo subsequently divides to produce twins, does the soul also divide, or has an all-knowing Deity placed two souls therein in the first place?

What of monstrous abortions? A 69-chromosomed abortion—a lump of tissue—has been described. Did it have a soul? A fertilized human ovum has been cultivated some weeks in a test tube. Did it possess a soul?

Even if the soul be limited to the brain, there are also cogent objections:

1. It introduces a new factor to heaven and earth, making the universe into a multiverse.

"The knowledge explosion of the past hundred years has given us a new vision of human destiny—of the world, of man, and of man's place and role in the world. It is evolutionary and monistic, showing us all reality as a self transforming continuous process, with no dualistic cleavage between soul and body, matter and mind, life and non-life, natural and supernatural. All phenomena, from worms to woman, from radiation to religion, are natural." [9]

2. An obvious objection is that, far from the soul animating the brain and outliving it, the brain in fact generates the soul, and when the brain dies, the soul dies.

3. The soul was centered in man at a time when the earth was centered in the universe, when the sun revolved about it and even stood still for Joshua.

But Galileo deposed man, who is now seen as a speck on a crumb of earth orbiting about a puny young star hurtling along an obscure sidestreet in a galacteal metropolis, itself no more than an atom among the galaxies of space. And possibly man may not even be alone in space.

Should man be eternal? At such cosmic conceit the stars disintegrate with laughter.

4. By what token can one deny a soul to the animals, of whom man is one and from whom he has evolved? At what stage of evolution was a soul paired with man's brain? Fifty thousand years ago? A million years ago?

An American pathologist and Sunday School teacher writes the following solution to this dilemma: ". . . just as there is evolution of the body, I believe that there could be an evolution of the soul and a continuance of this soul after death of the body . . . Perhaps the earliest forms of men did not possess a soul, or only had a very small spark of the essence which was later to develop into the soul. Ever since man has possessed reason and memory he has had the desire

*167*

for a future life . . ." [10] Similar views[11] are propounded by a Catholic Senior Lecturer in botany at the University of Newcastle.

5. There are two conditions under which human material has no brain.

a) The embryo is a product of two non-souled cells and a number of weeks of development must pass before recognizable brain tissue appears. Can a brain-centered soul animate an embryo before there is a brain to receive it?

b) Infants with anencephaly or hydranencephaly can live some weeks while devoid of any brain other than that exciting reflex behavior. They may even appear ostensibly normal until their inevitable death, and at autopsy there is found no cerebral hemispheres whatever, certainly less conscious brain than in a hen.

## Conclusion

The concept of an immortal soul gets no support on medical grounds; quite the reverse: medical and biological considerations place insuperable obstacles to regarding the immortal soul as anything other than a faintly ludicrous idea. Not only that, it is also a token of arrogance, of selfishness, that sees man as the darling of the universe. The fear of utter extinction and annihilation is insufficient to establish an immortality beyond the grave; some peoples welcome annihilation and seek it out. Immortality is anthropocentric conceit. The soul is a function of the brain in action; it lasts only as long as the brain functions.

This is a bleak outline. Man becomes no more than a wonderfully complex concatenation of reflex arcs, an animated machine, a robot, without free will. The behavior of the very young, the very old and the very sick is predictable, and in the final analysis, man is also predictable. Free will, freedom of decision, is an illusion. On the Chessboard of Life, man is a complex capricious Piece, and no more.

But humanists[12,13] discern something more in this man-centered scheme, something almost spiritual. Man cuts a noble, heroic figure in the world. To Man is assigned no less a role than that of being his own Saviour, his own Redeemer. A speck in the vastness of space, Man is at once its slave and its conqueror. Man has absorbed within him the qualities of the deities he has created: all that is good and all that is God. Entering the very heavens themselves, Man has fulfilled the prediction of Genesis: "And the Lord God said, Behold, the man is become as one of us . . ." (3:22).

Yet this too is insufficient. It offers nothing to the crippled, the dispossessed, the bereaved. For these, a soul is a great comfort. Consider the pathetic need of the Japanese mother who pictures the soul of her departed son in a garden paradise. In a couplet of unsurpassed sadness she muses

How far, I wonder, did he wander,
Chasing the dragon-flies today?

Let the lad have a soul. Grant a soul to all who wish it, all who need it. The soul exists for those who claim one; thinking makes it so. But this is not the grim soul of the humorless gospels. It is a playful soul, a soul of delight, not immortal, but postmortal, existing for as long as it is required, and extinguished when no longer conjured up by the imagination. The soul is poetry, a fabric of magic in a world of make-believe.

We end where we began, with dreams: dreams without dogma, souls without salvation.

The immortal soul is dead; long live the postmortal soul.

## REFERENCES

1. Needham, J. A. (1934): *A History of Embryology.* Cambridge University Press
2. DeWitt, F. (1959): *Journal of the History of Medicine,* 14; 360
3. Jakobovits, I. (1959): *Jewish Medical Ethics.* Philosophical Library, New York
4. Hertz, J. H. (1941): *A Book of Jewish Thoughts.* Office of Chief Rabbi, London
5. Greenberg, S., Ed. (1960): *A Modern Treasury of Jewish Thoughts.* Yoseloff, New York
6. Rabinowitz, L. I. (1951): *Out of the Depths.* Eagle Press, Johannesburg
   Rabinowitz, L. I. (1951): *Sparks from the Anvil.* Fieldhill Publishing Co., Johannesburg
   Rabinowitz, L. I. (1958): *Sabbath Light.* Bloch Publishing Co., New York
7. Clarke, E. (1962): *Transactions and Studies of the College of Physicians of Philadelphia,* 30:85
8. Gibson, W. C. (1962): *Journal of the American Medical Association,* 180: 944
9. Huxley, J. (1963) : *Nature,* 197:8
10. Smith, C. R. (1950): *The Physician Examines the Bible.* Philosophical Library, New York
11. Fothergill, P. G. (1961): *Evolution and Christians.* Longmans & Co., London
12. Lamont, C. (1961): *The Philosophy of Humanism.* Philosophical Library, New York
13. Huxley, J., Ed. (1961): *The Humanist Frame.* Allen & Unwin, London

# INDEX

## INDEX

apple, and Eve, 15
Aristarchus of Samos, 5
Aristobulus, 147
arteriosclerotic disease, in Asa, 43
artificial feeding, 129ff
artificial insemination, 107
artificial respiration, 44
Asa, King, 43
asthma, in Cain, 22
  in a child, 44
Astruc, Jean, 6
atash, 79
Atlantis, and Eden, 9
Augustine, 57, 161, 162
auscultation, 51
Avicenna, 164
azoospermia, 104

Baalzebub, Baalzebul, 68
Babel, babble of, 90
baboons, 11
bachelor, 108
Balaam's ass, 89
baldness, 44
banana, as forbidden fruit, 15
barley, 130
baths, medicinal, 46
bdellium, 8
beer, 130
bilharzia, 76
birthstools, 113, 115ff
bleeding disorders, 47, 138
blindness, 44, 53, 55, 63, 81, 92
blood, eating of, 69, 156
borborygmi, 51
bowels, sounds of, 51
Brahman, 163
breast feeding, 125ff
  by aquatic mammals, 6, 127
  in Adam, 19

breath, sweetening of, 62
breech delivery, 117
bubonic plague, 70
Buddha, 109, 163
  and Adam, 9
burial, 67, 144ff

Cabbalists, 158
Caesarian section, 119, 165
Cain, and Abel, 22ff
  and allergies, 22ff
  heredity, 18, 29ff
  mark of, 22, 32ff
camel's milk, 128, 129
Cangiamila, Francesco Emanuel, 165
cannibalism, 144
cardiac murmurs, 52
carminatives, 62
catecholamines, and forbidden fruit, 15
caul (obstetric), 122
caves, as tombs, 148
celibacy, 92, 108, 157, 161
Chemosh, 144
chickens, 11
childbirth, 108ff
chlorophyll, 7
cholera, 75
chorio-amniotic membranes, 122
Christ, and Adam, 30, 31
  birth, 109, 114
  case history, 47
  death, 31
  last words, 143
chromosomes, 30, 32
circumcision, 33, 40, 45, 59, 135, 136ff
cleanliness, 66
Code of Hammurabi, 40, 126

# INDEX

# INDEX